GREEN
ABOUT
GREEN

GREEN ABOUT GREEN

A Civilian in Military Life

Joseph Soeters

iUniverse, Inc.
Bloomington

Green about Green
A Civilian in Military Life.

iUniverse books may be ordered through booksellers or by contacting:

iUniverse
1663 Liberty Drive
Bloomington, IN 47403
www.iuniverse.com
1-800-Authors (1-800-288-4677)

ISBN: 978-1-4697-9502-7 (sc)
ISBN: 978-1-4697-9506-5 (ebk)

Printed in the United States of America

iUniverse rev. date: 03/12/2012

Contents

Aller voir nuit gravément aux idées reçues.
Go and see it for yourself, it will help you to rethink your ideas.

INTRODUCTION

Military organizations are something unique. The military dispatch their personnel to far-flung places throughout the world. These men and women are asked to risk their lives in the service of the state and in so doing often suffer a lot. Militaries are also unique because they frequently—for good reasons—conduct their business in an atmosphere of secrecy. But, sometimes a military organization does not want to reveal its actions because it is not always good at what it does, or because it now and then behaves unethically, especially towards the people in its area of operation.

For all these reasons studying the military is valuable and difficult at the same time. Researching the military is valuable because the use of violence, the military's core business, is probably one of the most unpredictable, impactful and dramatic forces in social dynamics. Further, a society's armed forces uses the taxpayer's money and hires citizens that could have earned their salaries elsewhere in the economy, under less threatening circumstances.

Studying the military is difficult because it is a world on its own, an island within society-at-large. Getting access, particularly if one is not a regular inhabitant of that island, usually is no easy game to play. On the other hand, if one is a regular inhabitant, it may not be easy to do research either, because the organization wants some control over the diffusion of information about itself. Hence, when it comes to the military, there is a societal and political push to know and an organizational tendency, however slight, to hide.

Therefore, I am most happy that I got the opportunity to visit a number of NATO—and UN-operations and other military sites, all over the world. My own research questions as well as requests from various national armed forces brought me there. Most of the

1

times I had to study—and report on—specific aspects of what was going on. But I was also simply looking around in order to try to understand the military logic. But I am not a military person, which makes me view things differently . . . Or makes me see different things . . .

These are my stories . . .

MATTER OF FACT, BUT NOT CYNICAL

At ISAF Headquarters in Kabul flags are invariably flown at half-mast. The national colours of the United States, the Netherlands, France, Germany, Canada, Rumania, and all the other participating countries form a dismal row. Over the last year there was an average monthly American casualty rate of 25, with a summer peak of fifty. On top of that there were the casualties other ISAF countries suffered.

Every dead serviceman means the start of the banner protocol with the banners of all the participating countries at half-mast for a period of four days to pay tribute to the deceased and, at the same time, to remind the inhabitants of the headquarters and visitors of the dangers of the situation outside the gate. You simply cannot miss the banners when going to the dining hall. It keeps the staff members on their toes and keenly aware of their responsibility.

There is danger lurking for everyone: for the infantryman at his outpost, but also for the officer on his way to headquarters. During our stay in Kabul, a suicide vehicle exploded at a five-hundred-yard distance from the main gate, resulting in three civilian dead and various wounded. At Minhad airbase in the Arab Emirates, while we were on our way to Afghanistan, we had already witnessed a so-called "ramp ceremony" for a recent Canadian casualty. Brian Richard Good, a forty-two-year-old trooper from Ottawa, as it turned out to be, had fallen victim to a road-side explosive.

Danger there may be, but there is also fear. Working in wartime is coping with fear, be it much or little, but seldom with sufficient fear. Too much fear paralyses and leads to passivity; on the other hand, too little fear makes people unconcerned or, worse, over-confident. It is not surprising, therefore, that the US Air Force has pointed at the dangers caused by thrill-seekers. Aristotle once said that a true hero is focused on achieving concrete aims, and stands midway between the extremes of carelessness and cowardice.

But where exactly is 'midway'? That kindles my interest as a researcher, perhaps because I am not a military person, yet still one who occasionally finds him self in an area of operations. In January 2009 I was at ISAF HQ in Kabul, and in Kandahar before that, to study the working of, in NATO jargon, the Effects-based Approach to Operations. The idea behind this doctrine is that it will no longer be possible to leave the control of operational activities to the commanders' judgement or instinct. Controlling the operations must be done more rationally, business-like, and based on figures and other information about results previously obtained, just like it is in trade and industry in the civilian world. But that is easier said than done. That is the reason for my stay in Kabul, together with two colleagues from the Netherlands Defence Academy: to study the working of that process in everyday reality. There we are, a lieutenant colonel, a reserve officer, and myself, a civilian whose working life had so far not been in the least dangerous. Until the day I came to Afghanistan.

The distance between Kabul Airport and Mission HQ is about 5 kilometres. That distance is covered in armoured military vehicles, which, to the layman, are unrecognizable as such. Prior to our journey we are thoroughly briefed by a corporal from the British unit that provides our transport. He speaks quickly and in an agitated manner, and his English is sometimes incomprehensible. What I will always remember is the cardboard notice he was waving in front of our eyes, which read 'White Toyota Corolla' and a car registration number. We were given the order—or urgent advice—to be on the lookout for this vehicle during our journey, as, among the many Corollas in the streets of Kabul, this Corolla was suspect, presumably carrying a suicide attacker. The announcement made us think of the roadside bombs and suicide attacks our soldiers in Uruzgan were up against.

It also reminded me of the young female officer commanding a German-Dutch convoy through Kabul in 2003. Two of the coaches had been badly damaged in a 'bomb-taxi' attack, which she had seen happening in her rearview mirror. She gave a penetrating and impressive account of the incident later on when addressing a class of students and I have had the pleasure of assisting her in the writing of her thesis on coping with fear. All this was going through my head during the British corporal's briefing. The atmosphere in the group, which had been rather relaxed at first, became one of nervous tension. Nobody could remember the registration number of the suspect suicide vehicle. During the journey one of us made an effort to look through the small, dusty windows, but there was very little to be seen. It was evening and in Kabul streets are dark and empty then. Everyone was relieved when we reached our destination. The briefing had taken longer that the journey itself. Those 5 kilometres through the dark and empty streets of Kabul had been done at record speed.

During my stay at HQ I bring this experience up a number of times, doubtlessly as an expression of my own fear. In Holland House I mention it to civilian employees like myself and to Dutch military personnel. To the military the subject is of little consequence, which is an attitude I have often come across. I have not heard reactions that are very different from, "When your time has come, you are in for it." It seems a way for soldiers to show that they are in control of themselves despite their fear. Naturally, they cry over the death of a colleague. Soldiers are just as frightened of what may happen—anyone who claims to have no fear is out of his mind—and they tend to get very emotional over the loss of a colleague. But they must stay on top of that emotion. You cannot fight fear by walking away from it neither by rushing forward like a bolting horse. No flight or fatalism, and no fight in a panic, but level-headedness and constraint, if possible, without cynicism. Being detached, with true emotions.

A Foreign Office employee immediately understands my point, when I tell her about the transport to and from the airport. The general feeling among HQ personnel is—or so she says—that it is better not to make use of official British transport. They have a reputation of tearing down the streets of Kabul in order to reduce the risk of attacks, sometimes with blaring sirens, antagonizing the local population because of the increased possibility of traffic accidents.

In the daytime the streets of Kabul are crowded, with youngsters trying to sell the merchandise they have displayed, with lorries carrying all sorts of cargo, and with passers-by and idle boys, who have nothing better to do. Accidents are likely to happen. The local population is aware of that and are cross about the additional danger brought to their streets, which increases the chances of attacks on these vehicles that are so easily recognizable to the insider. She would never make use of British transport, the colleague from the Foreign Office assures me.

I will certainly remember that. In the meantime it has come to my knowledge that there is also a Dutch transport service to the airport. When I have finished my work at HQ in a couple of days' time, I arrange this Dutch transport, which gives me a comfortable feeling anyway. Dutch servicemen appear to have a relaxed attitude towards their work. They carry arms, but they are not distinguishable as military. Their two vehicles drive at a leisurely speed through the streets of Kabul, while they watch every bend of the road carefully, and radio particulars to each other along the way. "In front on the left a car is pulling over . . . , but . . . . nothing wrong". This type of communication does not really make our journey a sightseeing trip, although there are a lot of interesting things to be seen in the streets. Daytime Kabul is lively and colourful. The atmosphere in the vehicle remains quiet, which is in accordance with the levelheaded impression the Dutch military make on us. In the past four months they have not experienced anything serious, apart from the odd Afghan's momentary attempt to cling to the bumper of one of the vehicles.

Functioning in wartime is coping with fear. With just enough fear, that is. Perhaps Dutch military are good at that, with a few exceptions, of course. During a previous tour in Uruzgan a 21-year-old sergeant in Kabul once had to drive his vehicle for four hours at 'dead-slow' speed, he told me in a remarkably light-hearted manner. While he came under fire he had been well instructed by a major, who was in the passenger seat, and who had also managed to keep his cool. When asked about the possibility of recurrence he answered promptly, referring to the incident as being 'part of the job'. I have also heard this before. Not all soldiers have this matter-of-factness. British military tend to be more nervous, I have perceived, which may be due to their extensive Northern Ireland experience. The Americans' reaction to fear is shooting, which is not so strange considering the reward placed on their heads.

My own level-headedness is somewhat restricted. What fascinates me, are missions abroad and the objectives to be reached. There is little I find more captivating. That is the reason why I have—quite voluntarily—been on 'missions' abroad to Bosnia, Kirghizia, Afghanistan, the Lebanon, Liberia, the Congo and Bolivia, either for field research or on a work visit. Prior to departure, I am invariably overcome by gloomy thought, fantasies really, about what may go wrong. Will I come back alive? In my thoughts danger comes from all directions: bombs, bullets and shells, of course, but also hijackings, diseases, poisonous snakes, and road accidents. My mind excels in conjuring up disaster scenarios, and I am sure people serving in the military will frown up my visions of fear. Fortunately, my presence in a war zone is always short-lived, and protected.

Soldiers in Afghanistan; they have my deepest respect.

A NEW FORMULA

"My company cars may have all the colours in the rainbow, except white . . ." The German manager of a brewery in Kinshasa speaks from the top of his voice at the birthday party of an embassy employee. He has provided the beer machines and there is a constant flow of Primus beer from their taps. He enjoys it the most himself, as the size of his belly testifies.

I do not understand his remark, "Why is that? What is wrong with white?" It is asking for a simple answer, for the subject of our talk is the UN's military mission in the Congo, and UN vehicles are painted white.

"Well, it would not be the first time that UN vehicles, these splendid four-wheel drives, get pelted with rocks . . . I have experienced that an angry mob surrounded such a jeep, tossed it on one side and pushed a burning cloth into its petrol tank. If such things happen, the vehicle catches fire instantaneously and you can only hope that the occupants will be able to get out alive."

It is not entirely clear to me whether he speaks from personal experience or whether it is one of his wild fantasies. I determine it to be the latter. It seems an outrageous idea to me that such things happen to UN, the United Nations, who are the representatives of the international community and guardians of human rights in the world. Still, the account has sparked the little flame of fear somewhere inside me.

The manager, speaking as a man of much experience and local knowledge, sounds too convincing for his story to be dismissed as drivel. He speaks of attempts at corruption he has had to withstand as a Western manager, right up to ministerial level. Such as the announcement of a new parking tax for his lorries, for example, amounting to 3 million dollars, which he received by mail from a newly appointed minister (perhaps solely meant to top up the latter's Swiss bank account?). He also mentions his tactics when there is a riot afoot. He builds a wall consisting of crates of Primus beer just outside the entrance of the brewery, with a "free beer to take away" note attached to it. It works, and the danger subsides . . .

The message is clear: here is a man who knows how to tell a story and whose stories, however fantastic and unlikely they may seem, are not to be disregarded just like that. "But why is it then that UN angers people so much?", I hesitate to ask.

"Well, it is rather clear, isn't it? In the eyes of the people in the street UN does not really seem to be doing much for them . . . a huge apparatus is in place, with rich foreigners driving in far too expensive cars, continuously racing past at high speed . . . What benefit are they to the local people? Take the Chinese, at least they fill up potholes in the roads, which you do not see UN personnel doing . . . The whole mission is going to implode . . . it will just stop . . . without anybody in the country noticing or caring."

Once again it becomes clear we are dealing with a man who does not take kindly to opposing views, as he is probably also not used to opposition in his own company. Moreover, as long as the profits of his breweries in the Congo are the highest of this worldwide concern, he will not get any complaints from the head office in Europe.

When his wife, who does not seem to have gained weight since early womanhood, comes to collect him for another party later elsewhere that same evening, he leaves me mesmerized and confused. I realize that in the coming week my two colleagues and myself, who have come to do research into the multinational control of the UN mission, will only be driven around in white vehicles.

The previous evening I had arrived at Kinshasa together with Bram, a civilian MoD colleague, ex-officer and currently reservist, and Maaike, recently appointed trainee and an air force general's daughter. We were met by a, perhaps too cheerful, defence attaché, who took us to our hotel, the only hotel where we were allowed to stay, because in the eyes of the embassy staff other hotels were too dangerous. They are bound to know these things. It was rather late when we had arrived at our hotel, but not too late for a beer. We made the liquid acquaintance of amber-coloured Tembo, blond Primus' great competitor, as we learnt the following day. The giant hotel had once been built by an American hotel chain and opened by the then dictator, Joseph Mobutu, who had taken such a fancy to the building that he declared it his property a few years later.

It is indeed a magnificent hotel, situated near the Congo River in the so-called embassy area in wonderfully cultured natural surroundings. Trees that almost fall over due to the heavy weight of red flowers add a parkland touch to the area. The international community and the Congolese elite both make use of this park and the hotel, albeit segregated. While we were having our belated drinks, a wedding party was going on, with beautiful young women in evening dresses and smart men in white tie, who arrived in a queue of Hummers, more than I have ever seen before in my life. Evidently, this was a party of the top layer of society, people in money they accumulated in whatever way.

Now I discuss the party at the embassy with Maaike and Bram, with a Tembo refill in large glasses, to be able to establish the difference in taste with Primus. I tell them what I have heard and ventilate my concerns. Bram laughs and waves them away . . . "Nonsense, there is nothing the matter here!" Maaike does not say much. I say I cannot seem to get my head around much of these stories, but that they appear to be important, also in the light of our research. I still cannot believe what I have heard at the party . . . UN, how can anyone be against it? My final thought is that the manager with the big stories is likely to be very much against any form of government intervention, therefore also opposed to intervention of the international authority residing in the UN building in New York.

"I cannot see it any other way", I conclude, "he may be a nutter, that guy . . . but his story is of importance . . . I feel it in my bones." Bram and Maaike hardly respond. Undoubtedly, they think I am rattling on a bit and perhaps see things differently.

Two days later our work has made reasonable progress and we have had extensive conversations with UN officials, including the deputy commander of the mission, a British general. After a rushed start of the interview ("What is this all about?"), he appears to be remarkably open and prepared to reflect. I cannot help mentioning the stories of the brewery manager to the general, as they are still on my mind. They do not startle the general, nor is his reaction non-committal. He knows the stories, probably not from his own experience, as he is relatively new to the mission. He tells about the glass that is half full and half empty, about progress made, but he also recognizes that the popularity of the mission in Kinshasa is not great. Kinshasa holds little danger for the people, and therefore the benefit of the mission is not clearly measurable. In the east where militias from inside the country and abroad still make life miserable for the local population, the mission is more popular, he thinks. Admittedly, also there UN vehicles are occasionally molested and it is there in particular that the UN mission receives criticism, because the Indian, Pakistani and Bangla Deshi soldiers are not always in time to protect the population when threatened with violence, or to restrain the regular army. What is remarkable is the general's ability to discuss the mission, and consequently his own activities, with so much honesty and detachment.

The theme of UN's reputation keeps haunting us during the talks. Gradually it is becoming clearer that it does not go without saying that UN has managed to acquire a positive position within the country's society and politics, despite the ten-year presence in the country, the largest budget, and the highest numbers of troops UN has ever been able to muster. This realization culminates at the end of the second day of our research.

We have arranged to meet—much later than planned—a Swiss colonel, who is the mission's Public Information Officer. His arrival is rather overdue, because he has had to attend an unexpected meeting with the President of the Republic on behalf of UN that afternoon. That meeting turns out to be the subject of our talk, also quite contrary to the planning. The Swiss speaks fluent English, but sometimes a word has escaped him, and I cannot place the French or German equivalents he uses instead . . . Are we both too tired? Anyway, the Swiss appears to be an emotional person.

He gives his account of the meeting he attended as UN representative a few hours before, in which the President announced the departure of the mission. The term would be negotiable, but it would be appropriate for UN to announce its exit strategy on the occasion of the 50th anniversary of the nation's independence. It would even be more appropriate if the withdrawal of troops would effectively start on that very day. The anniversary was in seven months' time, which would leave UN ample time to make plans.

The Swiss officer is visibly moved when he is telling this. He also makes mention of the French Ambassador's reaction during that meeting when he said the Congo was not ready yet for the ending of the mission. "The country may well have reached its 50th anniversary, most of the population will not," he had ventured to say in protest. The remark was ill received by the President, which he had clearly shown to the people present. It had given them a fright.

This goes to explain the Swiss' emotional reaction. He thinks the mission is nowhere near completion and that in this way all the good work will come to nothing, rendering his eighteen-month stay virtually useless. That is his personal frustration, nobody is eager to see all his work so openly reviled. It is unclear to what extent the Swiss has also become apprehensive about the developments. He estimates that politicians will mobilize the street, if necessary . . . and then, all of a sudden, we hear the same story about the angry mob and the white UN vehicles from him. After approximately two hours a sudden sob marks the end of the conversation. "This is enough . . .", he says. Bram prompts another question, to which no answer is given. The conversation is over.

We are quiet on our way back to the hotel. The sob has clearly affected Maaike, but Bram is unperturbed and positive, although he would not go so far as say, "Don't think too much of it, there is nothing going on here". Twice I heard the story of that angry crowd attacking UN vehicles from people who could know, and it does not let go of me.

In my hotel room I switch on the TV and search for the national French channel. It comes as no surprise that I have tuned in on a report of the meeting of this afternoon. The reporting is unbiassed, which should leave the viewer unimpressed. But Western ambassadors have not been interviewed, least of all the French ambassador, of course. The ambassador of Ivory Coast, a diminutive figure in a small hat, expresses his views, which are in line with what the President of the Republic stated previously. This is a touch of African solidarity, clearly.

The UN has been in the country for a considerable length of time, even as long ago as the first few years after the independence, and it is about time for the Congo to stand on its own legs. There is not much wrong with that idea. That is how quickly my opinion has changed in the meantime.

Then I switch to a music channel, just as I did the days before. It is a moment of relaxation and a moment to sample something of the local musical culture. The previous days had been somewhat disappointing with many video clips of gospel choirs and orchestras normally found on a religious TV channel. But tonight is different with a video clip that appears to last for more than a quarter of an hour.

It shows six bare-chested men in black leather trousers, dancing to riveting music in the twilight of the evening. Quite entertaining. Every minute there are more male dancers and the dancing is getting more exciting. Then, although a minority, women join in, all wearing the same uniform. The dancers are positioned in a V-shape, a tribal version I had seen develop spontaneously on a previous occasion at a party in South Africa.

Suddenly the dancers wield burning torches, and the scene takes a more ominous turn when a white jeep slowly comes into view and enters the crowd. The dancers surround the vehicle, and the view of the occupants of the vehicle is what the camera shows next. What they can only see are the faces of the crowd with torches in their hands, looking into the vehicle. The faces have taken on an angry expression by now (or is it just my imagination?). The music gets more and more exciting and the scene seems to be going on endlessly, until the windscreen of the vehicle is smashed in. That is when the clip ends.

With a quicker pulse than I normally have I switch off the TV. I have seen enough. Showing this video clip is an incitement to violence. Thus the President gets his way, if necessary. Is this a first warning in case UN may not have fully grasped the announcement made that afternoon? And what is the time frame: seven months or this week? In the latter case I will be there as a witness. Fear grabs me by the throat. Before I go out with Bram and Maaike to have a pizza somewhere, I hide the light-blue UN diary I bought in New York with so much pride in my suitcase and lock it. I realize the cowardice of the act, but it is cowardice without consequences for others, which I consider to be admissible.

While we are having our pizza I tell Bram and Maaike what I saw on TV. They look at me in utter disbelief, thinking I must have lost my marbles. Maybe I have, maybe not.

The next day the Swedish director of the civilian branch of the mission has little time for me. There are meetings to attend. However, we do manage to discuss events of the previous day in a good half hour. The cool Swede is not overly impressed, and certainly not afraid. He finds the events very 'interesting', and is curious about further developments.

What follows are talks with women for whom working for UN is their hearts' desire. They are cosmopolitan, there is no other word for it, have parents from different countries, speak perfect English and French, and have lived, studied and worked all over the world. For one of them the personnel members she met during other missions have become her children. Substitutes, in fact, which the photographs displayed above her desk bear witness to, and which she speaks of with great enthusiasm.

For another woman, a female Barack Obama look-alike, with a Nigerian father and a French mother, working for UN is a kind of life-fulfilment. She has a hearty laugh and is full of the work she does for UN, which focuses on the attitude of UN personnel towards the local population. On that score the UN mission has a bad reputation, which makes her work important. And she really is important: there is no general who does not know her and speak about her without respect.

The approach to the work she does is a very judicial one, which is not surprising for someone with a law degree from Harvard. She advises unit commanders joining the mission to take care that the predominantly male personnel do not get involved in any way with the local population. Not with women, because of the obvious risk of collateral damage due to sex, as 'boys will be boys', and not with men and women, because of the danger of corruption. The rule is: whoever goes against the rules will be charged.

The fact that such a position leads to the isolation of the heavily protected UN compounds is a drawback, which she readily agrees with. But there is no other way. I ask her whether she has ever been a judge. She has not, but she may well be, one day. I tell her she reminds me of my eldest niece, the star of the family, who has just become a judge. I meant it as a compliment and that is how she takes it. Her laugh is heartier than ever, and that is how I take it.

She has risen to her feet to signal that time is up. It has already taken longer than intended. Still seated, I ask her about her vision of the future of the country and the mission. Again that laugh, "Well, there is not much else to say than that all signals are red . . . . things are not going well, but still . . . you see, just like religious people believe in life after death, I believe in the future of this country . . . there are no indications whatsoever that everything will be all right, but still I believe in it . . ." She spreads her arms wide, her dress fanning out . . . charisma turned human. I look up at her . . . I am overwhelmed . . . I do, too.

The next day my work is almost finished. Bram and Maaike will stay for another week and travel to the East of the country to study the more operational activities of the UN brigades. While the war was raging in the East, in one decade, three to four million people were killed, and many more women and girls violated. And still the violence is not over yet, which explains the continued presence of UN troops. At an earlier moment I had already mentioned that I would not be joining them. One week is enough for me, to the utter disgust of anthropologists and other researchers that claim that a considerable amount of time must necessarily be spent in an area to be able to say anything about it. Perhaps they are right, but I prefer to decide for myself. A week of *Blitzfieldwork*, a term coined by others which I have gladly borrowed, is more my style.

After an exceptionally short night I went to see Bart and Maaike off at the airport. They will go back to sleep as soon as they are airborne. They will be all right, they assure me. What else is possible? I stay behind and still have a long day ahead of me. My flight will leave for Europe in the evening. I still do not know how to get to the airport. The embassy staff, who have been such excellent hosts, have so far not said anything conclusive about it. Although it is still early, I am beginning to feel somewhat uncomfortable. We agreed that I would be collected with my luggage at 10 o'clock, and that they would take me to the Dutch Embassy, where I hope to have a number of additonal talks, particularly with Congolese employees working there. These are the people that may know, because they read Lingalese newspapers and listen to the radio stations. But they are all too busy to talk to me. All I can do is send them an email with questions once I am back in the Netherlands. The ambassador herself is also too busy, as a delegation of the Dutch Parliament will shortly be visiting the embassy. Fortunately, we have been able to speak with her deputy a number of times in the previous days.

The hours pass slowly, but time goes more quickly when the deputy defence attaché,—in the absence of his superior who was seriously taken ill a few days earlier—takes me out to have lunch together and to see a number of art galleries, at my request. It is wonderful art, but too expensive and too bulky to take home. Still I decide not to let this chance slip away and to buy a small painting, featuring a pop singer advertising Primus beer. The picture attracts me: the text on it reads *"Lele ya sika"*, which approximately means 'a new formula'. The German gallery owner, who has lived in the country for over forty years, must ask her local gallery assistants about it. After all those years, Lingala is still a mystery to her.

Over dinner my host asks me about my transport arrangements to the airport. That question startles me! I answer that I do not know, meanwhile telling myself it will be all right. Then there is a hesitant affirmative on the part of my pensive host. He grabs his cell phone and, quick as a flash, manages to settle matters in my favour. This evening the permanent embassy driver will take me to the airport in his Mercedes Benz jeep. I do not have to worry, because the car is armoured and . . . not white. That afternoon we pay a visit to the Defence Attaché, who is sick at home. He believes to have contracted malaria and will be repatriated for diagnosis and treatment the day after my departure. His tour in the Congo has almost come to an end and he has had just about enough of the country and his posting there . . . for more reasons than he can explain. My deduction is: he has had too much of the tropics, too much of shady politics, of a colder atmosphere at the embassy than a military person is used to, and his insufficient knowledge of French . . . Indeed, time for him to move on to a new post, which I have already gathered from his words.

Not long after that Eric, the embassy driver, shows up in the Mercedes. A real *Kinois*, he knows the route like the back of his hand, which inspires confidence. He does not need a baseball bat on the back seat, as I have seen in the cars of European nationals, to solve possible problems he may encounter in the street. It is still light when we leave. The first few kilometres through streets in the town centre, which have become familiar to me, go rather quickly. Gradually the route becomes unknown, dark, and busier, as we are approaching the cité's, Eric explains. They are popular residential areas that resemble in some way the South-African townships. The difference is that we drive right through them, whereas the townships in South Africa are usually situated at a distance from the main routes.

To the keen observer, it looks nice and pleasant. There are small fires everywhere for roasting chicken, outdoor cafes, small shops in ramshackle buildings . . . and people milling about and talking, the women wearing newly-washed and pressed colourful garments. This is the mystery of Africa: there is poverty all over the continent, but women look as if ready to attend High Mass any moment of the day.

But there is poverty, devastating poverty, like communicating vessels connected with the lines of Hummers cruising through this town. The Kinshasa of the embassy district is not the Kinshasa of the cité's, but there is a connection. And it has become worse; *'Kinshasa La Belle'* has turned into *'Kinshasa La Poubelle'*, a de-generation from beauty to garbage tip.

Sometimes the car has to pull up because of the confrontation between the crowdedness of the cité and the procession of four-wheel drives heading for the airport. When we stop we are instantly surrounded by people, predominantly young men, with bland, curious, or angry expressions. "What is your business here?", "Why do you have what we do not?" My mind goes back to the video clip I saw a couple of days earlier and there are striking similarities. Only the music and the torches are absent. Eric puts my mind slightly at ease, *"C'est normal, on arrivera toute suite."* We will be there soon.

I can only relax once I am on board the airplane. The large bottle of Primus I paid a lot of money for at the airport is empty, but has not given me the calmness I was hoping for. Real peace of mind comes when we are airborne and I am certain I do not have to go back to or traverse the cité. Only then do I have time for my neighbour.

She is a woman from Seoul, who has given support to the Christian Korean mission station as a Korean-French interpreter. She does that every year and she knows the country, so she has not wondered about things as much as I have. We try to guess each other's age, an entertaining but not entirely harmless social game for people to play during their first meeting. "It is hard to guess a white man's age", she says evasively. The age of Asian men is easier to guess. But it goes well, it soon appears that we are about the same age. The conversation is gathering steam and we discover a mutual interest. She tells about her mission work and I am an eager listener. Her experiences are worthwhile, her opinions somewhat less. She makes deprecating comments about the country and its inhabitants, but her formulations are controlled. She cannot be caught saying anything racist.

Gradually religion enters her story and very soon it is more than I can stomach. I decide to reduce her missionary side and enhance her human side by giving her the opportunity to compare the story of Jesus with other world religions. Obviously she is quite prepared for that question and instead of putting the Jesus story into perspective, as was my expectation, she offers, in very fluent French, an unshakable profession of her faith intended to emphasize its superiority. I give up, which does not go unnoticed. "If you find me tiresome . . .", but I am too polite to contradict and say that it is time to get some sleep, meanwhile pulling the Air France blanket over my head.

On arrival in Paris I try to get out of the aircraft as quickly as I can. I have had enough of the Congo for the time being. The Korean woman, with whom I have had no further conversation apart from a polite *"Bien dormi?"*, walks passed me. Then she turns around and we shake hands. "Have a safe trip". "Yes, you too." We both realize Jesus has stood between us. However, still thinking of the female Barack Obama look-alike of the UN mission, I do believe. What is a human being without faith? What is UN without belief in . . . ?

An unexpected low

It is 10 o'clock in the evening and there is a cool breeze in the streets of Baku. The air of the Caspian Sea forces itself upon you, but it has a pleasant, natural smell despite the endless row of oil platforms along the coastline we saw from our aircraft. In the former Soviet Union they were never mindful of the environment. We are on board a Hercules and on our way from Brussels to Kabul, the centre of the ISAF mission in Afghanistan, and we are making a stopover in the capital of Azerbedjhan. The Hercules, one of many in the Belgian Air Force, transports cargo to the mission area, especially parcel post containing tangible tokens of homefront affection. On board there is also a random group of military personnel and civilians, on their way to Afghanistan for a variety of reasons.

Jan is a doctor on a six-week tour to provide first-line health care to Belgian soldiers at Kabul military airport. Valerie and Jeanne are veterinarians, Rico is a radio technician, and Danielle and I are two civilian employees in the military, travelling to the area to do research. My position is particularly special: not only am I a civilian, but I am also a Dutchman. Yet my presence does not give rise to many questions. Asking questions does not come natural to Belgians, and, besides that, the story that I originate from the Belgian-Dutch border area and am therefore part Belgian goes down well with Belgians. Valerie and Jeanne were a surprise to me. Vets are unknown in the Dutch armed forces, in fact they have been since the time of Napoleon Bonaparte. Belgium still employs a number of them in order to guarantee a sufficient level of hygiene in the various barracks and compounds. No matter how you look at it: bacteria are animals, too. Valerie and Jeanne are travelling to Afghanistan to assess the situation there. With these people, whose acquaintance we have only made that morning, we walk through the streets of the historic city centre. Hanging about in the hotel all night was not a very appealing thought, we had decided after dinner.

The streets were quiet, and there was less to be seen than we had anticipated, but the blend of Soviet-Russian and Ottoman architecture and atmosphere was intriguing. Curious and hungry for the unknown I take the lead and walk in front, but not alone, keeping contact with the rest. I point my finger at what I see and continuously converse with my travelling companions, my face turned towards them. I point at the ramparts, the palm trees, the lighted stalls of the evening vendors . . . it is a marvelous sight, which I want to convey to the others, almost yelling.

What I am not aware of is the danger lurking in these streets, unknown to Belgians and Dutchmen. I am approaching that danger, unknowingly . . . . Suddenly the ground gives way under my feet and I feel like a cartoon figure, legs dangling in the air, or like a cyclist on a bike without pedals. One more touch of something I grab, but cannot get hold of, too little, too late. I fall . . . and fall . . . and fall . . . and land with a thud on my back, flattened, dizzy, stars, just like in a cartoon. I feel instant pain and I am unable to move. I can still think clearly as my head has not touched anything, fortunately. Where, for heaven's sake, have I landed?

I hear the excited voices and shouts of the others, tearing down the same steps I have fallen down. The steps lead to the basement of a small shop. Jan is down first and, being a doctor, he takes the initiative and starts checking my legs and feet. Despite the shock everything is still in good working order, which is a relief to everyone, most of all to me, despite the acute pain. My companions try to make me sit up, but to no avail. In the meantime the shop door opens and out comes the probable shop owner, gesturing and shouting that we should scram. Jan tries to explain the situation, upon which the door closes again. This may be the local contribution to casualty assistance, which is: making light of things.

After more than a quarter of an hour I manage to get up, as the shock symptoms have decreased. Supported by Jan on one side and by Danielle on the other I manage to make my way up to street level again. We take a taxi back to the hotel. Once we are in my room Danielle and Jan help me take off my clothes and shoes and I have to undergo a thorough medical inspection by Jan. It is clear that my back is worst, black and blue and extremely painful. Jan is afraid one of the discs has been fractured, but after close examination and asking me questions he deduces that that is fortunately not the case. "You have a serious contusion", and, noticing the puzzled look on my face, he continues, "that is what you Dutch call bruising, I believe." They help me to bed and set my alarm clock. He gives me some painkillers to help me through the night. Reveille for our departure for Kabul is at 7 o'clock the next morning, and I have no idea what tomorrow will bring.

The night has not been very pleasant, with much tossing and turning, causing me a lot of pain. Setting the alarm clock had not been necessary for I was never fast asleep. I manage to get dressed and go downstairs unaided, but I have made up my mind: I am not going to Kabul with the others. That is the first thing I tell my travel companions and the aircrew when I join them at breakfast. In the meantime the pilots have already heard my story, and obviously they are not happy. Jan makes an effort at persuading me, saying, "In Kabul I can keep an eye on you all the time." But I do not feel like going, so I say, "Surely you cannot take invalids into an area of operations." In military circles this sounds convincing. Danielle is disappointed and she will miss her colleague, as we have not spent very much time on the preparation of the research. It seems we are about to pay for this neglect. However, a short chinwag cheers her up again. Within a couple of minutes' time we are able to exchange ideas and thoughts in a way that will be workable for her.

For the time being the pilots' minds are less at ease. They will have to continue their journey without a registered passenger, who will have to be flown back to Brussels as well. To what extent will the ministry in Brussels, and perhaps also the ministry in the Hague, have to be informed about this problem? Ever since the Hercules disaster at Eindhoven Airport an accurate passenger list has been more important than ever. The pilots know this better than anybody else. I am anxiously waiting for the outcome, because I want to go back home as soon as possible. Whether this is at all possible is still unclear.

Then 27-year-old Johnny, the captain of the crew, speaks up. Johnny is from Liege and is named after Johnny Halliday, the Walloon-French rock star his mother was so fond of that she gave her son that name as a token of her silent admiration for the star. The situation is obviously on Johnny's mind, but he does not want any ado. In two days' time he will be back in Baku with the Hercules, and back in Brussels after three days. That is also going to be my itinerary. When his co-pilot ventures to suggest that clearance should be applied for first, Johhny resolutely responds with, "Captain's decision".

Without speaking, I am very indebted to him. I admire his courage and youthful decisiveness. I agree with Johnny that there should be no questions. These two days in Kabul with a painful back I will survive.

Two days later the aircraft with Johhny and his aircrew returns from Kabul, but without my travel companions and without Danielle, who is going to stay in the area. Making an effort at showing an interest in me, Johhny enquires about my health. "I am OK", I assure him.

The next day we arrive at the airport and I drag myself up the aircraft steps. I can manage, but not easily. In the cargo area of the Hercules there is a Peugeot mini-van in the middle surrounded by a large quantity of scattered metal chests. The loadmaster indicates where he wants me. Especially for me they have put up a kind of stretcher at the height of about 1 m 60, which will be my living space for the next 8 hours, fortunately lying on my back. I suddenly remember that during the Vietnam War the Hercules was designed for the transport of wounded personnel, how appropriate!

I still have to try to lift myself up to the height of roughly one and a half metres. With a little help I manage by using several crates as stepping-stones. Even with a painful back it is possible. When I am stretched out I take a few more painkillers and hope that I do not have to go for a pee, which is a tall order in a Hercules anyway.

The eight hours pass while I am in a painful slumber. It is a quiet journey, which sadly brings back to memory the Hercules' flight of a Dutch armed forces musical band, which ended so disastrously at Eindhoven airport some years ago.

The next day I have been able to arrange an appointment at my local hospital, where the news of my mishap has already preceded me. The doctors have been informed. Photographs are made and I am told to wait in the hall. The doctor steps into the hall and, when he sees me, starts yelling. Even before I enter the consultation room I know the diagnosis, "You have broken your backbone. You should never have traveled in this condition. Irresponsible. You could have been paralyzed."

I am startled. I had not expected that. Thinking back of my climbing efforts to get on the stretcher in the aircraft, I now realise it might very well have gone totally wrong. "With an injury like this one should always go the a local hospital to have one's photographs taken. This kind of fracture can never be diagnosed from the outside. Do you promise never to do this again?"

Bowing my head, I solemnly promise.

Baptism of Fire

A coach takes us from Beirut Airport to Southern Lebanon. Together with Danielle I share transport with Belgian soldiers, some of whom are going to be stationed at a hospital and others are a mine disposal team. They are part of UNIFIL, the UN mission that, over the last few decades, has endeavoured to maintain the peace in the border region with Israel. Not overly successfully, it must be added. Violations of territory from both sides occur on a day-to-day basis and the war is never far away. Peacekeeping is a long-term issue, especially where it concerns the interface between Israel and the Lebanon. Danielle and I have come to study the daily life and work of soldiers on this mission.

The first hour of our journey the scenery makes a pleasant impression. The Mediterranean looks beautiful and peaceful, and the hills on the opposite side are blossoming. There is a lovely smell in the air when we halt for sanitary reasons. In the streets we see commercial posters with a strong Western signature. The photo models, advertising perfumes, watches, and cars, are just as scantily dressed and as beautiful as they are back home. Only the colour of their skin and their facial features may be slightly different from what we see back home every day.

What we see here changes gradually. It is not so much the scenery: what changes is the posters. The photo models have disappeared from the posters rather suddenly. They now show bearded men in black garments and black turbans. We know them from images from Iran; they are the same brand of believers. The small regional capital, *Little Teheran*, lies close at hand. The messages are in Arabic, but for the benefit of visitors an English translation has been added.

The intense animosity of the announcements is startling and I cannot remember having ever seen anything like it. Israel can be attacked any moment now is what the posters seem to make more than clear. 'The Israelis have not seen nothing yet'. To make the assertions all the more tangible, more and more pictures and realistic models of missiles, ready to be launched, gradually appear in the street scene. The projected outcome is a sinking naval vessel as a result of a direct hit, or a school reduced to rubble. However impotent UN may seem, they are not here for nothing. We absorb it all, tacitly.

On arrival in the camp we are briefed about the situation. Special emphasis is put on the danger of unexploded ordnance from the most recent Israeli action, serving as a kind of border protection for the Israelis. These mines are a major problem for the international contingency, but even more for the local population. The Belgians, in fact, do little else here than neutralize these explosives, and they are here to give patients the medical care not provided by the local services. Belgian dentists have drawn many a local tooth. Their work is highly appreciated, but it also causes victims. Only recently three Belgian members of a mine-clearing team were blown up due to the displacement of mines to a previously cleared area, as a result of heavy rainfall and a mudslide. That is the reason why we are not allowed to leave the compound unescorted.

The allocation of accommodation is what comes next. Being one of the few women in the company of many men, Danielle is given a place to sleep in an outhouse she has to share with two servicewomen. Fortunately she has a fixed bed, a luxury I shall have to do without, as a man in a men's world. Due to the rotation of shifts there are more people in the camp than space allows. That is why additional tents have been put up containing collapsible beds, one of which I may choose for myself. I find myself in a huge tent, which is also the temporary abode of most of my travel companions, whom I recognize by their young faces. I find a bed in the back of the tent, because I do not want to intrude upon the soldiers who already seem acquainted with each other.

As the evening progresses it has started to rain and the temperature has dropped steadily. We are in the mountains now and no longer in the pleasant sea climate. Rainwater flows through the tents and it is severely cold. Just like everyone else I quickly submerge into my duvet, with cold, wet feet.

Only the next morning does it dawn on me who my tent companions are. It is a Belgian Para-commando unit, elite soldiers whose exploits we have heard about so often in the rich Belgian colonial past. The most recent deployment was ten years ago, at the time of the Rwandan genocide, when a group of ten of them were ambushed and murdered after they had surrendered. To their own utter annoyance and that of the Canadian commander of the UN mission there, the Paras were immediately withdrawn by the responsible Belgian politicians.

Their departure facilitated the genocide, which was the intention of the ambush and subsequent massacre. The militants had indeed made a careful calculation. Ever since this incident the Belgian Paras have never really been deployed again. Later, in his memoirs, the Canadian General Romeo Dallaire portrayed the Belgian politicians involved in the decision to pull out as 'cowards'. The comparison with the Dutch blue-helmets in Bosnia is striking: Belgium, it appears, has its own 'Srebrenica'.

My Para tent companions may finally come into action again, albeit only around the camp and the hospital, for the protection of the personnel, as these youngsters claim with aplomb. It is obvious that these elite soldiers consider doing these guard and security tasks as beneath their dignity. When they notice I am a Dutchman they ask me questions about the possibilities of applying for the Dutch army. That army, they say, does the real work in Afghanistan: the work they have also been trained for, but are never allowed to put into practice.

For these boys the Rwandan tragedy does not ring a bell. At that time they were still running about in shorts. Despite their modest tasks, the weaponry they are issued with that morning is impressive. The rifles that emerge from the crates are almost as tall as they are, and they handle them with pride. So far I am not really impressed and Danielle and I decide to get cracking with our interviews.

We start with soldiers from the most senior ranks to the lowest ones, which makes our first day of work pass quickly. But before the day is done we have dinner outside the gate accompanied by two military policemen, called marechaussee, whose acquaintance we have made during the journey. They know the places to go to, for they come here for one week every couple of weeks to discuss disciplinary matters with the commanding officer. As is customary in Belgium, the duo consists of a Fleming and a Walloon, which means that we communicate in French. They know a diner just outside the camp, where they serve a delicious Mezze, naturally without alcohol in this part of the country. It was an offer we could not refuse.

Danielle, who has been my companion on a number of these trips, cannot fully enjoy the moment and is nervous, which is so unlike her. This young Belgian-Italian woman is always cheerful, pleasant and stable, but the posters flanking the roads we traveled seem to have unsettled her. She does not trust the waiters in the diner, and when there is a sudden loud bang outside, she is totally upset. The Belgian policemen, with their agonizing stories of criminal Belgian soldiers, try to calm her down, rather unsuccessfully. The pleasant atmosphere of the evening has subsided; we will not be dining out again in the days to come.

Two days later a trip to mission HQ also turns into a stressful experience. There has been an attack on Spanish UNIFIL soldiers and all transport is immediately ordered to stay inside. We have to hurry back to the Belgian camp in our little army-green Peugeot, wearing our flack-jacks. This is not protective enough for Danielle; she also puts on her helmet, which is a ludicrous sight, not only to me, but also to her self. We can still laugh about it, but it is not really funny. Our little Peugeot is not exactly what you could call an armoured vehicle.

After the dinner that concludes the first day of work I retire to my place to sleep at the back of the tent. It has become considerably more crowded compared to yesterday. The number of people seems to have doubled, as the rifles lying between the beds are of almost bodily proportion. Every Para has a buddy now, but I am all alone, slightly uncomfortable. Despite this I have a good night's sleep. A day or two later there is a brief rollcall for the Paras. It is an important moment and from a distance I witness the issue of ammunition, belts that can be fed straight into the rifle for instant use. Proud as children they go about their work and when they notice my presence some of them approach me to show me their toys. "Let Hezbollah or anybody else try and come near you, we'll protect you. You are safe with us!", they say encouragingly. Although I am trying hard not to, I look askance.

As always I am a champion in devising disaster scenarios. Noticing my hesitation, one of the Paras says, "Perhaps now you think it's not as safe as it seems." I make a faint attempt at responding, but what the boy said has struck home. I know it occasionally happened with the Americans, the British—and with who else I do not know—that someone runs amok and fires indiscriminately at own troops. This can easily happen when someone goes berserk, as arms and ammunition are always close at hand. In the Dutch camps I have visited in Bosnia and Afghanistan there are clear instructions about emptying weapons on returning from patrols. Still, the weapons are kept close at hand.

Simultaneously I realize that I am the odd one out in this tent, the civvy, the Dutchman . . . and when I put my foot wrong in this group I will be the painted bird. The very thought grabs me by the throat and will give me sleepless nights. I could claim another place to sleep, but that does not seem to have any chance of success. Moreover, it would set me apart as a scared rabbit. I still have some sense of honour. I decide to invest more into my relation with the boys, talk more with them, and say the right things. A voice inside me tells me I am such a jerk that these things do not come naturally with me.

So I play my trusted trump card again. I am from the Dutch-Belgian border region, and perhaps I know more about

Belgium that many a native Belgian does, especially because I grew up very close to the language divide. I know just as much about the Walloons as about the Flemish and there are not a great many Belgians that can say the same. I know how to give this story credibility, and someone passes me another trump card. One of the boys asks me whether I am a journalist, and his question conceals the respect for journalism that can only have been rammed into him during military training. I grasp the opportunity and reply, "Sort of . . . I write reports, not really for newspapers, but still . . ."

This observation is registered in meaningful silence. Obviously the public image of the Paras is a topic of conversation within the unit. After my two trump cards have been played I gradually regain my composure, especially when I take a keener interest in their video games. It dawns on me: the unrest I felt is because of me and about me, and not about them. They have not brought it about. Slowly I regain my calm again, I am happy to conclude. Good boy!

The sun is rising on the last day of our stay in the camp. Our work went well and we have gathered enough material for our 'reports'. Shortly before our departure for Beyruth Airport I go to the lavatories. Standing in one of the toilets I hear a few loud bangs, which I immediately recognize as rifle fire. Now look what is happening, I am thinking to myself, but I also have the impression that it is not very serious, it simply cannot be . . . It is hard for people to believe the worst has come.

I go outside to hear what has happened. Young Hezbollah sympathizers have just driven by in a minivan and fired a few shots in the air. Bullets were whizzing past as a welcoming for the newly arrived troops. This happens regularly when new troops have arrived, I hear.

At the gate I see one of my erstwhile tent companions on guard duty. He saw the minivan drive by just in front of him, with Lebanese youngsters firing into the air with their Kalashnikovs. He is totally upset and angry with everything and everybody. "Why am I not wearing a flak-jack? Where is my body armour? Where was the CO? Why is it that nobody tells me anything? I could have been dead!"

It is clear he has received his baptism of fire, and despite all the training, armament and audacity it has not been easy for him. My baptism of fire was in the loo, but that was at a distance, which is easy for me to say, as it is so often.

THE MYSTERIOUS OTHER

"For those who have intestinal problems, there is a toilet on your utmost right. That one is exclusively for people with defecation problems and if you follow that instruction, other people will not get infected." The person who is speaking is a Swedish NCO, giving the standard briefing to newly arrived service personnel. We have arrived at Camp Clara, the compound of the bi-national Irish-Swedish Rapid Reaction Force of the UNAMIL mission to Liberia in Western Africa.

The location of the camp is a former holiday resort near the ocean, close to the capital Monrovia, with swimming pools, a golf course, a huge hotel, and separate holiday villas. However, during the civil war the place was reduced to rubble, to which the jungle climate has also contributed. All in all, the site makes an apocalyptic impression. Not much of the infrastructure is left intact. Due to the civil war engulfing the entire population, but especially due to warlords terrorizing that population, there is a UN presence here. That is also why we are here.

We are flown in together with a group of Swedish military personnel, who all have different reasons for visiting their colleagues in Africa. Our travelling party comprises a Swedish general, who has come to inspect the progress of the mission and the Swedish contribution. I had been asked by two civilian colleagues from Stockholm to accompany them in order to study the cooperation between Swedish and Irish servicemen in the area of operations. Apparently there was enough cause for such a study. Despite the comparable political ideology of the two countries and the comparable contribution to UN peace support operations, their soldiers do not seem to get on so well.

For the time being we are among the Swedish, on the right-hand side of the camp. Everything is well arranged there, of which the separate toilet for those who suffer from diarrhea is just an example. The canteen looks smarter than any other one I have ever seen in an area of operations, and we immediately realize that the food is excellent and always fresh. Deer steak with red currants—a Christmas dinner!—served in the tropics. The food is always fresh, because leftovers are destroyed immediately after dinnertime. This is to the utter dismay of the hired Liberian personnel, because in Liberia food is never thrown away. Before dinner we must wash our hands twice, using water from a tap, and with an alcoholic gel, and under the close inspection of the Swedish. In Swedish care nobody falls ill.

That is a different matter with the Irish, the Swedes say in mockery. There, entire platoons are put out of action due to stomach and intestinal complaints; so planned patrols are simply cancelled. The Irish occupy the other side of the camp, practically out of sight. They sleep in dilapedated tents with airco installations that were in good working order once, which is a 'real' blessing in the tropical sun. The partition between Swedes and Irish is almost complete.

At one time while we are having dinner with the Irish, the differences are striking. There are facilities for washing one's hands, but no one uses them. In contrast to Ireland's sad potato shortages (or 'potato famine') centuries ago, there are now potatoes in abundance. The vegetables and meat are overcooked and the Irish eat from worn plates and mucky tablecloths. There is also a lot of noise. It is no small wonder that hardly any Swede ever makes use of the Irish canteen. Nor does it happen the other way.

Although both contingents belong to the same organic unit—the Rapid Reaction Force—there is hardly any cooperation, except by some officers on the operational staff. There are some Swedish and Irish staff members, who share a small office. Efforts have been made to plan joint patrols, but they appeared futile due to the frequent illness of the Irish soldiers when they have to go out. The Swedes mention this with a mixture of vexation and ridicule.

It is obvious that the Swedes have mixed feelings about their colleagues. Swedish soldiers tell stories about Irish soldiers getting involved with some black Venuses at the entrance of the camp. Clearly, these are horny men at the gate committing a deadly sin. Other stories tell of Irish soldiers cutting a hole in the perimeter fence to smuggle stolen woodcarving from the nearby hotel into the camp to decorate their own pub. In the eyes of the Swedes the Irish really did anything God and the UN had strictly forbidden. Fortunately, the Swedish commanders had managed to put a stop to these practices, "One should not be allowed to say, but they are a kind of hooligans, vandals, whose English is almost unintelligible!"

The Irish hardly know about these qualifications. They see the Swedish as professional soldiers, but rather dull, but they do not express it like that. The Irish think they are better at communicating, whoever with, because they have "the gift of the gab", as one of them puts it. Indeed, that is not something you would attribute to the Swedes.

For the locals of Monrovia there is a difference, too. They take more kindly to the Irish, because these soldiers are more inclined to talk to them. The Irish also hand on old, discarded kit to the inhabitants, and during their weekly round of sports they seem to take an interest in the fortunes of the families living in the cottages near the running track.

Not entirely unnoticed by the locals, the Swedes have been advised to keep the contact with the local population as limited as possible, also during sports activities. That will only lead to corruption and nasty diseases. Discarded things, such as TVs, chairs, couches, do not find their way to the Liberian population, bur are carefully packed and sent back to Sweden, to be dumped as garbage there. What Liberian should you give it to, anyway? That would only lead to inequality and corruption. Better, then, not to give anything to anyone, which is an attitude that is little understood in Africa.

The Swedes have one great asset. The handsome, fair-haired, and young men tanned in the tropical sun, in their robust, white vehicles—beardless Vikings—have a great attraction. Surely they have a high standard of professionalism and technical knowledge and skills, and they live up to that image. At the same time the host-nationals—with ill-disguised regret and jealousy—perceive them as untouchable. To many Africans there is always something enviable about the colour white and white skin, or else . . . something to love and to hate . . .

With this in mind it is not so strange that neither the Irish nor the Swedes play a significant role in this mission. They constitute the reserve forces of the mission, ready to take action when things go wrong, for instance, when there are demonstrations in the town. Then they make a huge impression with their modern vehicles. Sometimes they go on two-week long-range patrols in the hinterland, a kind of expedition through the jungle. A thorough preparation is required, because these big, heavy vehicles get stuck in the mud easily. That is why a tow truck is part of the convoy.

Normally one of the two countries mounts such a long-range patrol on its own, but sometimes a combined expedition is sent on its way, but that is the exception to the rule. However, on a daily basis, the real work in the street—manning roadblocks and checkpoints—is done by others, notably Nigerian soldiers, who are familiar with the languages, the daily business, and the way people behave in the streets of African countries. Moreover, they know better what to do when passers-by point at former war criminals, rapists, and murderers, who are now cabbies driving by in their yellow Nissan cars. That is, they do nothing at all!?

Integration in every-day life is the best remedy to achieve post-conflict reconciliation. That may be the reason why Liberia is doing rather well at the moment. Instead of widespread revenge there is the actual recovery of mutual relations and reconstruction, thanks to the female President, Dr Ellen Johnson Sirleaf, and perhaps also thanks to the company of Indian Women's Military Police. That does not mean that suffering has come to an end: there is still an emphatic requirement for healing among the population.

UN missions have a many-sided composition, as there are always many contributing countries. That goes well as long as every country is given its own tasks and area of operations. Because of this division of work there is no constant need for cooperation. But if two contingents are really stuck with each other, as the Swedish and Irish military are at Camp Clara, working and living together is by no means self-evident. There is one exception: the Irish Pub, which is open three nights a week. It is run by the Irish and frequented by the Swedes. They are regular customers, who never miss an opportunity to go there.

The separation of minds remains even when large tins of Guinness are opened. The silent Swedes are seated at the long tables on the right, whereas the boisterous Irishmen occupy the rest of the room. Sweden still has a predominantly male conscript army: among the Irish soldiers there are several young girls with red hair, who were recruited and trained as professional soldiers at a very young age. The pretty girls go from one man to the next, without any of them touching them.

One of the girls is also in charge of the music and the dance floor fills up quickly, all the more when the volume is turned up for Celtic technofolk. All the while there is an abundant flow of Guinness. The Irish know how to be lively, and they know how to handle their booze. They are certainly not dull, whereas the Swedes strictly abide by the two-can rule, the imposed daily ration of two tins of beer.

Even towards the end of the evening can the Swedes only sporadically be tempted to participate in the dancing, all by themselves, because who is there to dance with? All evening they have been looking askance at the Irish merrymakers, with a certain jealousy, it seems . . . resembling the way the women in black were ogling the fair-haired Swedish gods in their vehicles. But there is also disdain: in the opinion of the Swedes so much boozing is unacceptable during a mission. Secret admiration, envy, and disdain lie pretty close together, also for whites in Africa.

Together with Mats and Anne, my Swedish colleagues, who dragged me to the African jungle for this scene, I observe the spectacle. They fail to understand it, although observing the Irish drinking habits should remind them of the Mosebacke beer garden in Stockholm, where students and tourists are also known to hit the beer bottle.

The scene reminds me of the celebration of 'carnaval' in my city of birth, Maastricht, in the South of the Netherlands very close to Belgium. Absolutely convinced that this phenomenon would be to their liking, we sometimes invited people from 'above the main Dutch rivers' to get an impression of this typical southern event. How utterly disappointing it turned out to be when the fascination and the enjoyment were experienced so differently by the visitors. Northerners seemed to prefer 'a nice and quiet cup of coffee somewhere'. The evening was ruined. It was not wise to invite people unaccustomed to an event like this, although nowadays Northerners have grown accustomed to beerdrinking and partying since the rise of singers of Dutch popular songs, the success of our national football team, and the exuberant celebration of the Queen's Day.

I tell Mats and Anna about this. I try to explain the dynamics of the attractiveness and repulsiveness of the 'mysterious other person', with "carnaval" as a case study. I am not quite sure whether I succeed: I am not quite sure I fully understand it myself. While enjoying our last tin of Guinness, we leave it at that.

On the last day of our stay at Clara I have a conversation with the Swedish general, who accompanied us on our outward flight. We discuss a range of topics, but definitely also the relations between the Irish and Swedish soldiers. He makes no effort to make light of the phenomenon, but he appears to look upon it in rather a detached manner. It is a fundamental matter, and therefore not easy to change, if at all possible. In perfect English he summarizes, "The Irish have a problem with abortion, but not with prostitution. The Swedish people, on the other hand, have a problem with prostitution, but not with abortion." Just try to reconcile these points of view!

When I ask the local Irish commander for his reaction to rumours about an imminent Swedish withdrawal from the mission, he gives an unexpectedly gloomy reply, "If only we do not get Pakistani soldiers to replace them!"

Slob!

An ever-recurrent question when civilian defence personnel enter a mission is inevitably whether they should wear a military uniform or not. There is no standard policy, and I have personally experienced the two variants. In dangerous Afghanistan, however, the Dutch policy is simple: one enters the area as a military person, and there are no variants. That leaves little room for discussion when I am part of a team together with two other team members, a military lieutenant-colonel of the air force and a half-military lieutenant-colonel of the army reserves, together with whom I am to study in situ the effect-driven operations of the mission. We want to find out how and to what extent previous results play a role in decision-making during the mission.

One has to go to the Services Tailors in Utrecht where military uniform is issued to military personnel. Anyone who thinks this is a piece of cake could not be more mistaken. It takes at least half a day, and the total issue of kit forced upon you hardly fits in two supermarket trolleys. The retort made to my mild protestation was that the amount of kit is the same for everyone: "Last week some Members of Parliament received the same package. You are nothing special . . ."

We drove back to the office with the boot of the car filled with military stuff: overalls, sweaters, long underwear, T-shirts, socks, glasses, raincoat, bag, several pairs of boots, sun cream, insect spray, and, of course, a helmet and a gas mask. Flakjacks, too heavy to be constantly transported between Afghanistan and the Netherlands, would be issued on arrival in Afghanistan. I cannot place the gasmask: gas attacks, reminiscent of World War I, are an unknown phenomenon in Afghanistan. Perhaps that is the subconscious reason why I do not carry it about in my bag. I do not take it all too seriously.

When a day before departure I take my military luggage from the office to my house I suddenly discover that it does not contain the gasmask. That is what you get when you are not careful with your belongings! "Bother! This could cost me my trip to Afghanistan! At Eindhoven Airport they will undoubtedly go through my luggage with a fine tooth-comb . . . and when it is not complete, I will not be allowed to go." I only see misfortune coming my way, and so many weeks of preparation going down the drain.

Luckily, my son comes to my rescue and proposes to take me back to my office to collect the gasmask. It is past seven in the evening, and it crosses my mind that the office will be empty. Anyway, the suggestion is better than nothing, better than running the risk at Eindhoven of being refused to travel.

We arrive at the office building to find that the gates are indeed closed. To my relief I see open doors, presumably because the cleaners are at work. I cannot leave it at this, so I start climbing the fence. Necessity urges me on and I circumvent the fence in no time, like a monkey climbing a tree. My son, who is still behind the wheel, has never seen me that audacious. I am inside and the gas mask has soon been found, so, thank God, that is settled then. Afterwards I am told that I have committed a serious offence.

Uniform shows rank. That is the way it is in the army, but also in the police force and the fire service. So, as soon as I am told that I shall have to wear uniform the question arises what I will do with the rank temporarily bestowed on me. Shall I show it, as I am obliged to, or shall I dispense with it, because I do not really have that rank, let alone deserve it? I ponder and ponder and decide that I have not earned the rank and am therefore not allowed to strut around in borrowed plumage. There is one drawback: it would create a lack of distinction. That objection, I find, does not weigh up to the other argument.

I am quite happy with this argument when we have to wait at the Canadian transit camp Mirage in one of the Arab oil states, before we can proceed on our journey to Afghanistan. We are told that a Canadian Hercules carrying the remains of a dead soldier will shortly arrive. Before the flight back to Australia a 'ramp ceremony' will take place, which all of the military personnel currently present at the base are expected to attend. Each country will present itself separately. One of my travel companions whispers jokingly in my ear that, according to my rank, I will have to lead the group of Dutch military personnel.

The joke causes confusion; in any case, it does for me. This is not supposed to happen! I failed my admission tests as a conscript and I have never learnt marching drills, let alone giving commands in front of the troops. The confusion soon subsides when a major with operational experience takes the responsibility and starts to give instructions to the group, including my travel companions. I am ushered to a place among the civilians, most of them representatives from embassies in the oil state. More than ever I am conscious of my ambivalent, if not unclear, identity as a civilian in military uniform in an operational setting. I feel out of place here, or that is how I feel when the ceremony starts. The tribute to the dead young soldier is impressive, to the military as well as civilian spectator, and it removes negative feelings from my thoughts. "The soldier did not die in vain", is what we all sincerely hope.

At the HQ of the ISAF mission in Kabul I am beginning to feel at home, and I am getting used to wearing my uniform. Nevertheless, I have a remarkable experience at breakfast. When the Italians, with whom I shared the breakfast table, have left, I sit alone to finish my bacon and eggs, so there is room enough for a small woman wearing a US Air Force uniform. She joins me and she starts talking to me in an exaggerated, but very polite way, her sentences invariably beginning with "Sir". She appears to be pilot of the one but largest bombers in the world, with much operational experience. I marvel at the combination of the impression this tiny woman makes as a person and the actual work she does. Undoubtedly, her diminutive frame fits wonderfully well in the cramped space of the cockpit of her monstrous bomber.

I am not really comfortable. I have always looked upon bombing as a kind of porn of the military, without any human measure or emotion. Her exaggerated politeness is beginning to get on my nerves, so I make haste finishing my breakfast. When I get up from the table, ready to leave, she also gets up and salutes: "Have a nice day, General . . . !" I am perplexed, and extremely uneasy. I have no idea why this is. Then I realize I am wearing the VIP badge that serves to give me access everywhere. That must have been the cause of this scene.

This remarkable experience has been the start of a new working day. I go from meeting to meeting, across the entire camp, with Holland House in the centre for coffee breaks and moments of rest. While I am on my way to the next appointment, I notice a soldier observing me critically as he is walking towards me. I cannot distinguish his rank or nationality, but his vile look does not escape me. I decide not to give it too much thought, but it does make me conscious again of my uniform and my own person. The combination is somewhat strange, which the passer-by must have noticed, but he has soon disappeared out of sight, and I put the whole thing behind me.

The following day I have an appointment with a Dutch captain, whose specific task it is to register and analyze the results of the mission. These results or effects are then used as input for the follow-up plans. Important work, but not the kind of work every serviceman would enjoy doing, as the average soldier is more focused on action. When we meet there is instant recognition: he happens to be the soldier that was looking at me in such a disapproving way the day before. Instantly the penny also drops with him, and he tells me of his amazement at seeing such a slob walking about in the camp. A Dutchman, of all people! The term he uses amazes me and I—a rejected conscript—do not know yet that that term was traditionally used to denote young recruits who did not wear their uniform correctly. It was the customary denigrating way to instill discipline in these youngsters and to keep them in check. It was effective perhaps, but most unsympathetic.

With me it is the same: it is also about my uniform, as I have gathered. I have trespassed on two counts, he says wryly. I was not wearing my beret correctly, and the pieces of string to tighten my trouser legs at the bottom were missing. I was not aware of either of these charges, and I am surprised by the tone in his voice. Perhaps others have also noticed the two 'problems', but whether politeness forbade them to mention it, I cannot say. Not wearing badges of rank was also totally amiss, he says in a self-satisfied manner. Wearing my heart on my sleeve is my third flaw. I explain why I decided not to show myself in borrowed plumage. I also express my eagerness to learn how to wear the beret in the correct fashion and how to tie the pieces of string to make the trouser legs look bulgy. I may as well learn these skills while I can.

All in all, my critic makes a rather cheerless impression. In his eyes there is very little in this mission that meets the required standard, although, surprisingly, he finds the work he does interesting. He states that during his stay in Kabul he has been able to witness good progress, and just like me, he believes the work is important. Without knowledge of obtained results it is hard to change course, he says. At least some professional pride exudes from his words and during the interview he states that we as outsiders really understand the essence of the matter.

This is an unexpected compliment coming from this wry mouth. But the politics are wrong, and about the mission he is only moderately positive. That overshadows everything. He will be glad to be away from here, leave the service, and go into early retirement. Then he will take his wife to Portugal and live in their second house. The prospect does him good, this is practically the only thing that does. I register his way of speaking with mixed feelings. I am surprised at his dissatisfaction, while there is not so much cause for it, in my opinion. Of course, I am also a bit jealous about his early retirement after so few years of active service in not so very dangerous working circumstances. But, I suddenly think, he will come to regret that in Portugal he will no longer be able to call anybody a slob. That is a pleasure he will never have again.

Call me a slob? What do you take me for, you sod!

¡El pueblo unido!

The taste of cocktails and wraps is good at Ocean Drive, the main boulevard separating Miami from the sea. The barmaids are beautiful, the hotels are characteristically built in art deco style, and the view is simply 'awesome'. This is the very spot made famous by endless American television series. Still I find it all a bit disappointing, slightly boring even. The damned Eurofile in me tells me that the boulevards of the French Riviera are more beautiful. Freddy, my colleague and travel companion, on the other hand, is less deprecating about the scenery and relishes it while he still can. Tomorrow we will find ourselves in different circumstances, poorer, but no less interesting.

El Alto is indeed poorer and more interesting. The next day we drive through this elevated city for the poor—not very different from a ghetto—on our way to the Bolivian capital, La Paz. There is no military mission in Bolivia, nor is there a civil war raging, but the atmosphere is *"unheimisch"*, unsettling. When the situation goes off the handle, these roads are used for mass demonstrations, and for installing roadblocks, making it impossible for vehicles and coaches to pass. Then the army will be deployed to re-establish law and order, resulting, as it did on one occasion, in dozens of casualties because of the live rounds fired at the civilians. It happened on a Sunday, Sunday, Bloody Sunday, not in Northern Ireland this time, but in Bolivia, in La Paz and Cochabamba. This situation could not go on, and the government had to go, and the military had to change.

On the invitation of colleagues from the Canadian Royal Military Academy we have come here to present proposals for the reorganization of the educational programme, and everything

43

around it, of the Bolivian Collegio Militar. The presentation of these proposals will take place at a conference organized especially for this occasion. Traditionally the Americans are asked for advice, but not this time. There is currently a different political wind blowing in Bolivia, and the Canadians have been asked to provide support, and they have asked us to join in. In Anglo-Saxon thinking the Dutch and the Canadians are closest to each other, where human rights, use of force, post-conflict reconstruction of society, and related matters are concerned. The Americans still do not consider this their core military business and the policy of President Bush is not popular in Latin America, not to mention the British, who have yet to come to terms with their own Sunday, Bloody Sunday.

The air in La Paz is special: high up in the mountains it is thin, sunny and fresh. This sensation intensifies when after our arrival the reception committee takes us on a trip to Lake Titica, the lake at the highest altitude in the world and famous for its reed boats. We feel like tourists, and that is what we really are. But that feeling does not last, because on our return to La Paz we are taken to a barracks for dinner. There we meet the people that come from far to attend the conference for the first time.

We are surprised at the high numbers of people present, and about their attire. It looks like a folklore festival with many representatives of social communities attending the conference in the typical Bolivian colours and traditional types of dress. This is a representative collection of the *asuntos indigenos* en *pueblos originarios* that exist in the country, the original inhabitants of the country dispersed over so many tribes and groups within the population.

We also hear the first bizarre accounts of how relations between the various groups within the population, particularly between the white and indigenous elements, resonate in the training courses for officers. The courses are accessible for everyone with the right qualifications, of course. In practice this means that predominantly boys—no girls, but that is gradually changing—from originally European families follow the officers' course and become officers. Europeans are 30% of the entire population, but almost 100% of the officers' corps.

The conscripts, on the other hand, are predominantly from indigenous stock, and some come from a variety of Indian tribes. Whenever it occurs that a boy with an indigenous background is admitted to the *Collegio*, he does not have a very cushy life if he prides himself on his origin. That is why within months after their entry most of them make their names sound more Spanish. Rodrigues, Rivera, or Morales may sound well at the Collegio, but at home parents are not pleased with such a name change when their son comes home for Christmas for the first time, feeling they have partly lost him due to the change of name.

During dinner it soon becomes clear to us that this is felt as a grave injustice. There is tension all around. Conversation partners tell us that on that particular Sunday officers—of European stock—gave orders to native conscripts to fire at demonstrators and strikers of their own indigenous groups. This is told in a relatively quiet way, but underneath there is fuming rage. Even with limited knowledge of the Spanish language I manage to grasp that much.

The next day the conference is opened by our delegation leader, a Canadian colonel, and by a Bolivian general. The latter emphasizes the importance of the Bolivian army. There is still resentment about the fact that the country has no direct access to the ocean, resulting in the on-going tense relation with neighbouring Chili.

Above all the general stresses the necessity of change in the army. He cannot do very much else in the light of the changed political relations. The audience is numerous and divided into two groups of about 100 persons each. One group consists of military personnel—men—in colourful vaudeville uniforms, summoned to be present at the conference. The other group consists of many representatives of groups within society—men and women—who we met at the chili con carne dinner the day before. They are here because of their conviction.

Freddy is the first speaker at the conference and he talks about the policy on diversity in the Dutch armed forces. He always does that very well: he is a real performer. He has extensive knowledge about the subject, has roots in the Dutch Antilles, plays a role in the policy-making circuit at the ministry, has an easy laugh and is entertaining. "My name is Freddy, and my favourite band is Helen Ready" is the Frank Zappa quotation he always uses when introducing himself. His story is well received, although it is not entirely clear whether every part of his message has been understood. There is no denying there is a language problem and, although the interpreters are doing excellent work, it is doubtful whether everything that has been said has really come across.

The remainder of the evening passes as could be expected, with nothing special happening. In the afternoon we as foreign visitors are free to go to La Paz and act as tourists. The representatives of the two groups continue their discussions in smaller groups, the contents of which, much to our relief, will remain a mystery to us. After all, one cannot help being human.

The next day begins in the same way as the previous one. There are some presentations from members of our Canadian-Dutch delegation, followed by presentations from the Bolivian political and military top brass themselves. Striking for all present is the contribution from Brock Ipakanawat, a lecturer at the First Nations University in Canada, which focuses on—and provides a platform for—the indigenous inhabitants of that country, the redskins, as he, the son of one, puts it plainly. His account of the gallantry of Red Indian soldiers serving in the Canadian army, who fought on the beaches of Normandy, is very impressive. He does not conceal the sad fact that the greatest hero came to a bad end after the war. Is that the fate of the redskins? Of war veterans? Of both?

As the morning progresses, there is increasing turmoil. Despite the language barrier the dissatisfaction of the *indigenos* is clearly perceivable. Then the bomb bursts. Fists are hammering on the table and there are shouts from all sides. It resembles Paris in 1968, much more colourful, but just as historical. The message appears to be: it just cannot go on like this. Discussion groups are planned again for the afternoon and the foreigners are exempted again . . . But they must hear what is discussed in the groups and they must take an active part in the discussion, angry spokespersons say, often women. It is clear that this riot cannot be quelled with soothing words. Our trip to one of the sights outside the town is cancelled. We are to take part in the discussion.

There are some Canadians that speak Spanish, so for them the lack of interpreters for the discussion groups is not a problem. For us it is more difficult, although with my smattering of Spitalian I am able to follow something of the discussions. It is the people against the military establishment . . . and the establishment must be silent and accept. That is what the relations are like now. The prospective elections and expected victory of Evo Morales have already announced themselves.

Evo Morales is the leader of the Indians—with a Spanish name—and the first presidential candidate in the history of Bolivia who knows how to unite all the indigenous groups of the population. *"El pueblo unido jama será vencido!"* A united people shall never be defeated. That old Chilean battle song of the 70s—so often sung, played, and translated—also pervades the air at this location. It is remarkable that the mode of speech, despite the sudden agitation every now and then, generally remains polite and respectful on both sides. Both parties realize that in the new Bolivia they will be stuck with each other. They will have to stand together.

The outcome of the discussions at the end of the afternoon is a plan for the next and final day of the conference. Two planned addresses by foreigners are cancelled, but mine is to take place, presumably because the title of my contribution indicates that the subject of my talk is the improvements of officer training and education. In an atmosphere that breathes change the title is an appropriate one, because it holds certain expectations. Instead of the cancelled contributions of members of my delegation the representatives of the various social groupings will make certain announcements. These declarations will be assembled and serve as input for the changes in the educational regime and programme at the academy.

When this agreement has been reached, the atmosphere returns to normal again. Only now does it strike me that there are no youngsters present at this gathering, even though they are at the centre of the discussions. That would be different in the

Netherlands, in Europe, and in the United States. I conclude I am not nervous about tomorrow, although I will be the only foreigner on stage. Remarkable.

The next morning my nerves are still under control. I really feel like going on stage, also because I have to. I decide to pay some extra attention to what I wear: a properly tied red necktie to go with a blue blazer, which is quite a difference with the previous days. I look like a preppy student, while that is not even remotely my style. I wear this outfit without really being aware of it. The realization will come later.

The morning session is chaired by a woman anthropologist from the university, by chance also the sister of the Secretary of *Asuntos Indiginos* and *Pueblos Originarios* Affairs. Consequently, she knows a lot about these matters, and she has a lot of support among the audience. According to the planning I am the first to perform.

My presentation deals with the systematic improvement of the Dutch officer training courses, and the ever-increasing emphasis on the broad approach to military action, with an understanding of, and interest for, cultural factors in areas of operations, human rights, human leadership, civil-military cooperation, and the importance of local participation in the development process. I also point at the role of the Srebrenica disaster in the implementation of these improvements, as it was a real turning point. I conclude by giving a list of points of interest that may be useful for the improvement of officer training courses all over the world. It is the only time I speak in general and do not refer to the Dutch example.

Later on I receive some criticism on exactly this point, because the Dutch experiences in Bosnia are a world apart from Bolivian reality, as the critics say. 'Srebrenica' does not affect people in Bolivia in any way. That is what you get when you have the best of intentions and do not want to sound patronizing.

There is some applause when I am finished and ready to leave the stage. I have acquitted myself of my task, but the chairperson has other plans. She asks me to take a seat at the table on the stage, in case later on there are questions from the audience. That is quite all right with me, but first there are the statements of the various social representatives. The speakers are the people in the colourful traditional garments, this time more men than women.

When all of them take their turn in saying their say, time is no factor of importance anymore. Their message is solely intended for their own supporters. Every speaker starts out in Spanish, which interpreters diligently translate for us. After some sentences, however, the interpreters give up. "The speaker now speaks an indigenous Indian language, which I do not know", is what I hear through my earphones. This is what happens throughout the morning, so that soon there is no need for earphones. Most of the military personnel present—officers—did not need them, but now they have to give up as well, the majority of them being European Bolivians.

Seated at the conference table I am getting more and more uneasy. Initially I am there on my own, but after some time other speakers join me when they are ready with their presentations. There are friendly nods, but that is all. The table starts filling up with speakers all dressed in garments Evo Morales, when elected President, was to make world famous. Foreman of the coca farmers, he always wears a waistcoat or a loose-fitting Andes sweater in public. At my table they all wear hats or caps as well.

I feel hopelessly out of place in the outfit of a failed member of a students' union. I am the total opposite of what is known as a snappy dresser, but I now look like a businessman in a business suit. Disguised in this way I feel like being an actor in the wrong play, or a civilian in a platoon of soldiers. No discussion follows, because there is no time left. The morning on that stage goes on endlessly. Freddy, who is in the audience with his camera, makes another photograph of this spectacle.

Afterwards, as I am leaving the stage, I ask the chairwoman whether she liked it. At least she is content. When I tell her that I thought I looked a bit quaint with these clothes on, she reacts in an indifferent, but not unkind, fashion . . . "No, that was no problem, really . . ." I just cannot believe it! "You have simply become part of our revolution", she says, smiling.

FACE PROTECTORS

In the dining hall of the Dutch camp in Bugonjo the young herrings and salmon taste well indeed. The days of Srebrenica are long gone, and the SFOR mission just after the turn of the century is not as demanding and enervating as UNPROFOR in the preceding years. The food is excellent; it is evident that it is given a lot of attention, because good food is of vital importance for soldiers, and for whom not? No wonder, there are busy and lively queues of people waiting to help themselves to a good meal. Among them I spot a ruby-red beauty dashing past. I cannot help asking my hosts who she is. "That is Jasna, one of the possible persons you will be speaking with. She is a local interpreter".

Froukje, a student from Utrecht University, and I have only just arrived here to study the role of interpreters during military operations. Therefore we have to interview interpreters hired locally. Naturally this can only be done at this location, the area of operations. However, in the days ahead we will not be able to talk with Jasna. We only see her pass by every now and then. She keeps herself to herself, or the military keep her away from us.

Initially not many people see the value of the role of interpreters during military operations as a research subject. The armed forces of European countries see interpreters as just an instrument that must be used. To the American and British military at that time, interpreters are just people of no particular relevance at all. Americans and British are fully convinced that everyone in the world understands and speaks English, no matter where military operations take place: in Iraq, Afghanistan, or Bosnia.

In Fort Leavenworth, the centre of U.S. military training in the vicinity of Kansas City, certain scenes are acted out, in which

American soldiers, while searching Iraqi villages, shout their directions and orders exclusively in English. When that proves ineffective, the hunt is on for a quivering local, who at least understands a little bit of English. That is not a hired interpreter, but just a frightened, captured person. That this is American procedure, and that it causes a lot of uncertainty on all sides, has only recently become clear to me. During a dinner an American two-star general had whispered in my ear that he would personally like to screen all the interpreters—a relatively small number—the Americans make use of in Bosnia, because "what it comes down to is that you cannot trust anyone".

The Netherlands army does things differently. Where the Americans only provide a company commander with an interpreter, no Dutch patrol deploys without an interpreter—even if the person in command is 'only a sergeant'. This is a world of difference in approach. The Dutch know that without knowledge of language in areas such as Bosnia, Iraq or Afghanistan one would be acting deaf and going around with blinkers on. When asked my American colleagues say that there is no money to spend on more interpreters. "No willingness to spend!", is my jeering reaction, quickly calculating for how many days one interpreter can be hired against the price of one missile!

Besides this unjust comparison of costs, for the Americans the security aspect—you cannot trust anyone—is paramount. Therefore, they try to enthuse American citizens with knowledge of the specific languages spoken in the operational area to apply for a job in the military, with money on offer. Knowledge of Serbo-Croat for the Balkans, Arab for Iraq, and Dari or Pashtun for Afghanistan, becomes lucrative business. Former asylum seekers are now deservedly appreciated because of their original identities.

In the Netherlands armed forces Dutch civilians with the former status of asylum seeker are also employed as interpreters. They receive a uniform and officer rank, which immediately leads to friction and jealousy. What have these people done to attain that rank? They are no more than 'civilians in uniform', aren't they? The two Dutch captains of Bosnian origin we talk to in the camp in Bugojno feel bothered. They do not feel comfortable with these reproaches. They are the interpreters that are used in the more difficult situations in which the more senior officers are involved. That appears to stir up illfeeling here and there.

The majority of interpreters is hired locally and are consequently no soldiers of the Dutch armed forces. In Bosnia there are just as many male as female interpreters, Serbs and Bosnians, predominantly young single men and women, former students that speak reasonably good English. It is difficult to get adult men, as most of them have either been killed or participated in acts of violence or other disturbances. That is why many women do this kind of work. They have to earn a living, because their husbands or possibly future husbands cannot. Besides, everyone agrees that the wages are good.

Local interpreters accompany foot patrols, attend meetings with local authorities, and give education at schools about the danger of roadside bombs and mines. Female interpreters are used when, in the execution of their tasks, Dutch soldiers come into contact with women, but not only then. Dubravka recounts how she was verbally humiliated and spat on when Dutch soldiers had to confer with the Mujahedin, the fundamentalist Muslim fighters from the Middle East, who had come to the Balkans to do their 'blessing' work. She was never frightened, though, as the Dutch gave her sufficient protection.

The interpreters are proud of their work and feel generally appreciated by their Dutch employers. They consider themselves more than just 'translation machines': they are cultural mediators trying to make the communication between the Dutch and the local community go more smoothly.

That is difficult enough, so the ritual of greeting people receives more attention than is customary in the Netherlands and a higher level of politeness is maintained. Nowhere else in the world is Dutch straightforwardness so 'appreciated' than in the Netherlands itself.

Sometimes there may be friction with the military men, who do not understand why a translation must either be so short, or sometimes so long. Particularly young and inexperienced soldiers become ill at ease in such circumstances, all the more when interpreters appear to have learnt Dutch on the way. They are people with linguistic skills, more than the average soldier. It is clear the interpreters have the knowledge that enables them to be in charge. According to a British writer, interpreters enable both parties to understand each other by repeating what it would have been to the interpreter's advantage for the other to have said. However smart that description may seem, it is too cynical and narrow-minded.

The Dutch benefit from what the interpreters may have to offer. Not only do the interpreters know the language and local customs, they also do their work in the mission for a longer period of time than the Dutch, whose tours are limited to six months. As a consequence the interpreters have extensive knowledge about what is going on in a mission area, who pulls the ropes in the region, and who is involved with whom. The memory of the military depends largely on that of the interpreters. Quite a number of Dutch military, therefore, largely depend on interpreters, officially but also privately sometimes. This may never lead to intimacies with female interpreters, and therefore the Dutch servicemen's quarters are out of bounds for the interpreters. This may sometimes seem a restriction to the servicemen, but also to the interpreters. This is a minor—and sometimes not so minor—discomfort.

In Bosnia, several years after Srebrenica, the mission is relatively relaxed. In Afghanistan, two years on, talks with local interpreters show a more forbidding picture. No Jasnas with auburn hair to be spotted there. Instead there are only single young men, who have university degrees and are fluent in English. They are interpreters for the money, but even more so for contributing to the reconstruction of the country. This is where idealism—besides "what else is there for me to do?"—plays an important role, for which they pay a high price. No one—no neighbours, no uncles or aunts, not even sisters or brothers—is to know that they work for the international coalition. So they change into other clothes when they leave the compound when their work is done. They take special care not to have their identity cards on them, because whoever is known as an interpreter for ISAF is a kidnapping target, and a kidnapped interpreter is a dead one. Generally the opponent leaves no doubt about that. Outside the camp interpreters have to merge with the masses, for their own good.

It does not cheer me up to listen to Qasim, Atiq and Hamid's stories, which they tell with a certain resignation. They have been used to a life of uncertainty all their lives, and know that nothing will ever be certain. In an Afghan's perception there is no party or institution that he can always rely on. Local interpreters are outsiders to their employers—the international military-, and their identity needs to be unknown to the local population, particularly the Taliban mingling among the population. In fact, local interpreters are strangers in their own country, their city, and their compound.

That Dutch soldiers do not always trust all the interpreters is borne out by the fact that the latter have to hand in their cell phones when entering the camp. Some time ago this became apparent when the camp in Uruzgan was thoroughly searched, because an interpreter who had been fired was thought to have entered the camp unauthorized and with evil intentions. A search of many hours proved unsuccessful: the alarm had been false.

Still Qasim, Atiq and Hamid are not dissatisfied about their work. They can mean a lot to the Dutch. Everything that is the order of the day in Bosnia also goes for Afghanistan, albeit to a higher degree. They facilitate the conversations by executing the usual greeting rituals with the slowness that accompanies every action here.

"Peace be with you, Sayid, and how are your children? How is their health? Is your family all right? May you be granted a long life." For a Dutchman a simple "good morning" would suffice.

Interpreters take care that the critical questions that Dutchmen pose do not sound so negative. Their translation usually begins with neutral or even positive remarks that—often serving as an introduction—were originally never made. Sometimes they convey apologies that were never uttered. "Sayid, I know it sounds discourteous, but the captain asks what is true about the stories that the construction of the bridge is not making much progress." That is why in the eyes of the soldiers and officers the translations are often incomprehensibly long.

When they have to converse with a woman, male interpreters take care not to be in view by standing behind a curtain. When a Dutch officer speaks with pride about the horse-riding lessons of his two daughters, interpreters tend not to translate that part. These matters are not discussed with strangers in Afghanistan: it is considered just as much a taboo as not believing in God. The interpreters see to it that in all these situations neither of the conversation partners loses face. That is essential: in many places in the world loss of face is much more detrimental than anything else. During missions in far-off regions interpreters are the real 'face protectors', more so than helmets, glasses, deserts shawls, or even weapons. After all, words—if chosen well—can silence guns.

FIGHTING FALCONS

Missions are not only carried out on land. The air is equally important: for transport—of troops and equipment—, for reconnaissance—what happens on the ground—, for showing the flag—to demonstrate one's presence—, and for close air support—to come to the rescue of people on the ground, who cannot extract themselves from hazardous situations. But, air operations are best known and most feared because of their possibilities to influence the course of conflicts by way of aerial bombardments.

With the exception of transport, the Dutch and Belgian F16s, stationed at Villafranca Airbase in Italy, are in principle ready to execute these roles. But within the framework of the SFOR mission, in the years after Screbrenica, they are primarily used for reconnaissance and for showing their presence as a kind of 'impression management'. This is the strong arm in the air.

From the airbase near Verona the aircraft take to the air in pairs, cross the Adriatic in two hours, circle over Bosnia for four hours, refuel in mid-air and then make the two-hour flight back and land safely at the airbase again. A full working day in a cramped space, but with the most fantastic view one can imagine.

"Taking care not to wet your flying suit while you are in the air is probably the most exciting aspect of such a flight", a pilot tells us while we are talking about his work during a working visit. The light-hearted nature of the remark surprises me, all the more when he continues by saying, "This is not the real work, of course." "What is it, then, for Heaven's sake?", I ask. "Well, when we do dog-fights over the North Sea in order to prepare ourselves well for the moment we meet face-to-face with the Russian or anybody else . . . The planes we fly are not called Fighting Falcons for nothing.

If I had wanted to fly in circles, I would have worked as a pilot for KLM, our national airline . . . then I would have had more room to myself in the cockpit and be surrounded by beautiful air hostesses, and I would have earned more . . ."

During the exercises there is no real fighting either, I think to myself, and whether these dogfights in the air will ever occur for real is rather unlikely. This is no more the era of Biggles or the Red Baron, the fighting aces of the Great War. It is clear where the pilot's interest lies: it is with the technical aspects of his task and with his skills as a fighter pilot, and not with the current political and operational context of his work. Even the unfortunate role of the Dutch F16s at the time of the fall of Srebrenica—withdrawn due to the workings of international politics when it really mattered—is left undiscussed.

The entire atmosphere in the Belgian-Dutch detachment does not remind one of a genuine mission abroad. There is hotel accommodation for the pilots and other personnel, from where a queue of vehicles departs for the airbase every morning. Only one or two of them may leave somewhat later, and drive faster, more daringly, and dangerously to the base. The air force is fond of flying low after all, the pilots add with a laugh.

Maintenance personnel see to it that the aircraft are in perfect condition—the F16 has only one engine that may not break down—, meteorologists and other specialists all do what they are assigned to do, and the pilots fly their daily sorties. It is an eight-to-five working day and in the evening there is time for relaxation. Everyone has his pizza or spaghetti in the restaurant, and a beer afterwards in the bar of the hotel, where the deployed personnel is staying. Beer is not allowed for the pilots, who have to take to the air the next day. For the others the atmosphere is more relaxed.

There is the odd case where things go slightly wrong. On one of our nights at the hotel I wake up because of somebody's yelling and roaming through the corridors in an inebriated state. After some stumbling, the yelling has ceased, and I return to sleep. The next day a Belgian maintenance mechanic is put on a plane home. That is his career gone out of the window for him. However light-hearted the atmosphere in Villafranca may be every now and then, such conduct is not condoned.

There is a different atmosphere at the American airbase at Manas, near Bishek, the capitol of Kirgizia. Here a Dutch-Danish F 16 squadron flies missions within the framework of Operation Enduring Freedom, the mission launched by the Americans to fight terrorists in Afghanistan. It is the European contribution to a mission, which is not particularly popular with the Europeans so shortly after 9/11. The base already existed, but has recently been renamed after the Chief of the New York Fire Department, Peter J Ganci, whose gallant conduct at the smoking ruins of the Twin Towers immortalized him.

From this base, as from Villafrance, F-16s fly in pairs, not over Bosnia this time, but over Afghanistan. The purpose of the air operations again is principally reconnaissance and 'showing the flag', making their presence known. Actual fighting is not necessary. The airbase commander at Manas tells us that the Dutch F-16s have not fired a single shot for months. Still, everything is different, more threatening. We are not accommodated together in a hotel, but in tents at the base. Everything is well arranged, but the tents are what they are. The security situation in this former Soviet republic is not such that Western military personnel on operational tasks can stay in a hotel. For some years in this young country, Muslim fundamentalists with Taliban leanings have been active, which explains why the entrance to the camp is heavily guarded.

The pilots abstain from making light-hearted remarks about their flights. They are apprehensive about the high mountains they must cross before entering Afghan airspace. There is still uncertainty about the F-16's single engine. "The Swiss are better off, they fly twin-engined F-18s, which is always safer . . ." "The Swiss are also richer," they add, with a modest laugh. "Above the Adriatic the F-16's single propulsion system may give way, but then you can eject and your parachute will enable you to land safely, so in most cases you can be picked up."

"Here, above those mountains, you are hopelessly lost. When you manage to land on those mountain crags it is unlikely anyone will ever come to your rescue. It is simply too far away and too inhospitable for search and rescue helicopters. Then you are done for." The pilots tell this with such seriousness that I have never heard before. They clearly see this as a risk factor, and the tense atmosphere during the briefing and the usual issue of the emergency rescue pack and pistol just before take-off goes to show how serious it is, at this location more than in the Mediterranean. I admire their courage and sangfroid.

In Bosnia as well as in Afghanistan these operational activities are no joke compared with what happened at other moments or what is still to happen. Just before the turn of the century, even before 9/11, Dutch F-16s took off from Italian soil and flew a series of bombing missions over Serbia. The capital Belgrade was heavily bombarded. Only the Americans and the British surpassed the number of sorties flown by the Netherlands air force during that campaign.

There were good intentions behind this—uncharacteristically Dutch—bellicose attitude, which was supported by both the political right and the left. The crisis in Kosovo had to be brought to a favourable conclusion, but most of all it was the intention of the Dutch Government to repair the damage done to the image of the Netherlands and its armed forces by the Srebrenica tragedy in this way. The Dutch cán fight was the message of this sabre-rattling. The pilots will not have chaffed about this.

Within the framework of the operations in Afghanistan the F-16s were soon transferred to Afghanistan itself, first to Kabul, and later to Kandahar. Then they do not have to cross these far-away mountains to reach the operational area. But there, together with the Apaches, they have got much more closely involved in the hostilities on the ground. These operations may be a far cry from 'dog fights' high up in the air; nevertheless, F-16s live up to their reputation of being spying, looming, and if necessary, fighting falcons.

Superstition, and other discomforts

We had arranged to meet in C terminal of Charles de Gaulle Airport in Paris. I flew from Amsterdam and Angele came from Brussels by train. When I arrive, she waves enthusiastically. "Finally the great day has come", she says.

It means much to her, this research trip to the West African country of Benin. She works as a researcher in Brussels and occupies herself with the living and study environment of African army and navy cadets at the military academy in Belgium. They are approximately a fifth part of the total number of students at the academy in Brussels, and all of them come from French-speaking Africa.

With this educational policy Belgium follows in the footsteps of its own colonial past and that of France, a country that still maintains close ties with its former colonies. France also trains large numbers of prospective officers from French-speaking Africa. The academies of Brussels and French St Cyr are completely in line on this. The same applies to research: Angele also does her research for and in France, and it is not for nothing that she speaks French, although her Flemish family name might suggest otherwise.

Some months earlier we had attended a workshop in Brussels where we discussed the provisional results of her research. Everyone was enthusiastic about her findings, which show how African students experience living and studying in Europe. Like everything else in life, these experiences are both positive and negative. But something was missing: how do these officers who have recently graduated fare when they return to their own country and their own armed forces? That is what Angele knew nothing about.

However, it was a known fact that students from the Democratic Republic of Congo often do not complete their training and education at Brussels or St Cyr. During or shortly after their study they run away and enter the world of illegal asylum seekers in Belgium or France, or whichever other country, perhaps America. Becoming an officer in the Congolese army does not appeal to them, because the salary is almost negligible, the army too erratic and violent, and politics too whimsical and dangerous. Youngsters, who study for that army, take their future into their own hands and vanish even before taking the exams. That is a setback for everyone involved in the educational process, and therefore the whole project with Congolese students has been discontinued.

Benin, that small country next to Nigeria, is a different story altogether. From a democratic point of view the country is an example for the rest of Africa, and a reasonable security is safeguarded in the streets. But there is certainly much poverty, and, as in so many development countries, the growth of the population still exceeds the economic growth. Despite the much applauded growth spurts it is not getting any better. Belgium has established close ties with this country, especially in military respect, because, as the story goes, the ambassadors of the two countries were 'neighbours' during UN meetings in New York, the simple reason being that the names of the two countries begin with 'Be'. For the Belgian armed forces this connection means that logistic support is given to Benin during peace missions, in which Belgium does not participate itself, and that Benin enables Belgian troops to do jungle training in Benin. Furthermore, Belgium provides opportunities for young officer-cadets from Benin to study in Brussels.

If we would like to know more about the reintegration of young African officers, graduated in Europe, in their own country and armed forces we should visit Benin. Very soon afterwards the decision was made that Angele and myself go there together. The outcome of that decision is our meeting at Paris airport about half a year later. Angele is very optimistic, "Now I will be able to see what those African students are talking about during our lengthy interviews . . . now I will be able to understand . . . you must have been there to really be able to talk about it . . . and write a thesis about it". Now I hear she has never set foot on African soil before.

While we are waiting for our flight to Africa we go through our programme. We will be assisted by defence personnel from the Belgian embassy at Cotonou, the capital of Benin. They have laid the contacts with the Benin armed forces, which have shown their willingness to assist. That is not surprising considering the fact that every year five to ten officers receive their training in Belgium at the expense of the Belgian taxpayer. So, understandably, there should be something in it for Belgium. The Benin army command has arranged for us to meet a sufficient number of relevant people: everyone who studied in Belgium, but also senior officers up to and including the Deputy Commander-in-Chief of the armed forces to sketch the broader context. Angele and I are content: so far, so good.

We chuckle when we read what it says about Benin in travel guides: the country is the cradle of the voodoo cult. Although Haiti is better known for it, the cult originates in Benin and has reached the Carribean by way of slave transports across the Atlantic. However hard the Christian and Islamic missionaries tried in the past, most people in Benin have persisted in that other faith. According to the travel guides, they see divine powers in animals, pythons for example, in trees, in small statues and amulets.

There is still little evidence of that yet when after our flight has landed we are met at Cotonou airport by Lambert, one of the Belgian defence personnel. Lambert appears to be a very amiable omnipotent, who will prove very helpful in the coming week. Like all the other Belgians there he is French-speaking, which is quite useful in such a francophonous African country. After checking in at our hotel he invites us for drinks at the veranda of his house. Together with him, his wife, Angele and I experience the wonderful sensation of being in the Walloon provinces of Belgium in a tropical setting. I owe the familiar feeling the French-speaking Belgian atmosphere gives me, as it does now, to my boyhood days in Maastricht, with the regular outings to nearby Liege—*La Ville Ardente,* the ardent city. Every now and then Lambert speaks to me in amicable Flemish. He is good at that, and he has to be as a Belgian officer. That is quite a relief for me, because the conversation in rapid French has already become rather a strain after one hour, *"très fatiguant"* indeed.

The next day commences with a waterless shower and an elevator that malfunctions when I am in it. Is that voodoo, I wonder? I put myself at ease again thinking it must be a typical discomfort of a development country. We start work at the headquarters with an interview with the deputy commander and a number of his colonels. One of them has large tribal scars on his skull and jaws, which is an unusual, rather frightening, sight. He would do well as the stereotype "bad guy" in a James Bond movie.

The conversation partners provide a picture of the training and education policy in the Benin military. We are made to understand that the Belgian contribution to that policy is greatly appreciated but, in essence, a very modest one. Officers of the Benin forces receive their training and education in numerous countries, not just in Belgium, or in France, the former colonial ruler of Benin, but also in Germany, America, and nowadays also in China. This project has gone on for decades, for our conversation partners—all in their fifties—studied abroad, one of them even took the course in Russian in the former Soviet Union.

Besides that, a large number of officers are trained and educated in the country itself. It is specifically brought to our attention that it is important to realize that no distinction is made between 'home-bred' officers and those who were educated abroad. Everyone is treated equal, according to the official rules and regulations the general is constantly quoting from. No one has an advantage over others, regardless of the high quality or specialist character of their education, and wherever it took place.

The general also repeatedly points at the so-called *harmonization* phase all officers have to go through after finishing their training and education. "Foreigners" have to become "Beninese" again and they need to get rid of possible adverse customs they may have picked up abroad, is the additional comment made jocularly. Hearing that everyone is made to toe the line again sounds rather ominous to us. If the study abroad has made the youngsters pretentious they should beware, and the careful listener immediately understands that these words refer to the power relations within the armed forces. The conversation ends in a cheerful and relaxed atmosphere, and the part of the conversation that was in French went reasonably well. It went *"super bien"*.

In our following interviews with the young officers that studied in Belgium, the conversation goes less smoothly. Even for Angele not everything is easy to follow. *"Ils machent les mots"*, she says, "They chew the words, they drawl". Probably because of their enthusiasm and under the influence of their own tongue—*Fon*—they do not pronounce the French words accurately. So, a cacophony of sound arises, from which it is hard for a Dutchman to extract the contents. Also at the academy in Brussels there were problems of this nature, when teaching staff indicated that they could not fully understand the questions or remarks from their African students. Conversely, this was considered rather insulting by the African youngsters, as Angele had already gathered from her interviews in Brussels. This was one of the more negative points in their experiences.

Nonetheless the talks with the young officers are satisfying. They have sometimes come from far away, over a more than five-hundred-kilometre distance, on the boss' orders. They have been summoned to come to Cotonou for this purpose. Some conversations are done individually, some in groups. Sometimes the local beer is served during the talks, with the intention of the person who pays for them 'to loosen tongues'. The remark induces laughter all around. There is much laughter in Benin, certainly when something is said that has a deeper meaning. Could this also be an aspect of the voodoo tradition?

Angele is in charge, which she does to perfection. With her fair hair and white skin she is the epitomy of the 'white female' and she manages to use her feminine charm in such a manner that the conversations are successful where content and atmosphere are concerned. Much is gained from these conversations, and however hard it is to follow them sometimes, the essence does not escape us. This is mainly due to Angele's well-articulated and clear summaries of what has been said. She must be the perfect teacher. The young officers as well as myself are happy with it. Now everybody has an understanding of what has been said.

The young officers are content with the education in Brussels, although they have sometimes felt somewhat neglected by their Belgians hosts, but they are happy with the acquired knowledge in the field of construction engineering, electronics, meteorology, and political science. The only problem is they cannot sufficiently put their knowledge into practice in Benin. The equipment they have learnt to work with is not available to them. That is not only due to the lower level of development in Benin, but often also due to uncooperativeness. Although the Benin Air Force has meteorological instruments at its disposal, the meteorologist educated in Brussels is not allowed to work with them, because he is still too young, too insignificant.

The young officers had high expectations when they came back to Benin, and they thought they would be made to feel very welcome on their return from Brussels. What a disappointment was awaiting them! Also, when put in for promotion to higher posts, their specific knowledge is not taken into account. The senior officers make their decision as to who will be promoted only according to their own personal preferences. "When they like you, you have it made."

On being asked they unhesitatingly give the assurance that political orientation, or regional or religious background, plays no role of importance here. This fits nicely into the relatively good democratic tradition of Benin as it has developed since the country's independence. That is a totally different story in many other countries in Africa, where the working of politics often leads to war and violence.

The whimsical promotion procedure, however, makes them alert in the social contact with their bosses, the senior officers. When such a person asks something, even if he is not one's immediate superior, one must react instantly and drop everything else. That is something they are not at all used to in the Belgian army, at least not to that extent. *"Les chefs ici ont beaucoup plus de pouvoir qu'en Belgique"*. Bosses have much more power here than in Belgium.

Young officers speak with derision of *"La Beninoiserie"* when they talk about what, in their eyes, are the dysfunctional aspects of their organization. In general there is a generation gap between the young officers trained to be experts and their commanding officers, who lack this expertise but are bent on clinging to power whatever the cost. The whimsiness with which they do that is inherent to behaviour aimed at exercising power. Although the Beninese people are no strangers to things human, this is what is called a really serious clash between the different views of organizations. But there are still smiling faces all around, certainly when after the interview we all line up for a group photograph, with a present-day Marilyn Monroe beaming in the middle.

For dinner there is *poulette byciclette* on the menu, one of Benin's traditional dishes: grilled chicken with little, sinewy meat on its bones, the result of a lifetime of running ceaselessly across a farmyard. My memory tells me I liked the same dish better in Kinshasa. I discuss the results of the last few days with Angele and Lambert. The research makes steady progress and we are more than content. After some time the conversation changes direction and Angele and Lambert indulge themselves in astrological reflections together, which suddenly takes a very serious turn. This happens to my utter amazement. In this voodoo country my Belgian colleagues seem to be very serious about the signs of the zodiac. Fortunately, both Angele and I appear to be Sagittarius, which she is very content with. So am I, to be honest. "We go well together", she says, and then she sums up all kinds of combinations that also do or do not.

I am all ears. Lambert tells a story about a relative in the Ardennes, who had broken off her relationship, because their signs would not be a good match. A better example of a self-fulfilling prophecy will be hard to find. I am not making an effort to hide my scepsis, nor am I venting my doubts, because I cherish our mutual relationship far too much. Anyway, I can stomach a bit of Belgian *voodoo*.

The Chinese connection

A greater contrast as then in Shanghai I have rarely ever seen again. As the radiant centre of attention amongst a gathering of grey, pale gentlemen there was a young black lady with a proud smile, relishing the moment. The elderly gentlemen—in casual clothes and white sneakers—were stooping a little as they stood there watching the erect figure; they admired her choice of a black cocktail-dress, which added lustre to her dark complexion. I could see from a distance that the company knew each other. The opening reception of the conference about Armed Forces and Conflict Resolution had started.

Mussie and I had arrived the previous evening, and we were still somewhat drowsy as a result of jetlag. We were there at Mussie's own request, as he wanted to present his research findings at this location, right here in China, because this young researcher had been aware for years that one had better not bet all one's money on Europe, as it had gradually become the 'old world'.

His research was about the development of Eritrea in the period after the war with Etheopia, which had lasted for years on end. His interest lay principally with the reintegration of the so-called 'former fighters'. What is to be done with men that have been fighting a war—a trench war—for years and years? This is a constantly recurring problem when conflicts have been brought to an end, for which time and again new solutions are invented. In Eritrea the former fighters have been given employment in the civil service, but whether they are the best public servants a country could wish for remains to be seen. This invites further study, which is what Mussie has done for his promotion research. I was approached to supervise that study by doing field research, together with Mussie, in Ashmara, the capital of Eritrea. That was some time ago, and now we were here, in Shanghai.

The next day the conference was officially opened. The Chinese admiral that welcomed us could not resist showing us some slides intended to put the rise in Chinese defence spending into some perspective. The rise did not amount to much, and in comparison with US spending, the Chinese increase was really rather limited. The admiral did his utmost to convince the predominantly Western audience of his country's innocence. After this effort at presenting politics in an academic guise the conference could begin in earnest.

Mussie and I were planned for the afternoon. It soon appeared that the 'lady in black' we had seen at the opening reception was to chair our session. I had found out in the meantime that her name was Pela from Jamaica, who was doing her promotion research in New Zealand. The elderly gentlemen, who had stood around her to do her credit, were her professors from Waikato University. Pela was Jamaica to a T, the island we know from the world of sports and entertainment, strong, dashing, and vital.

When we assembled to proceed to the conference room, Pela and I met coincidently face to face. I was impressed like a fifteen-year-old schoolboy, which made me lose my words. I could not help uttering in superficial and clumsy English, "Are you prepared to do your job?" She ignored it. Our session went like clockwork. Mussie did a great job presenting his research findings; Pela was well in control with disarming charm. The professor in a wheelchair sitting in front got all her attention. She was right and truly "prepared to do the job".

The following day I had a conversation with Alba, who was a Professor of Anthroplogy in Rio de Janeiro, and a disenchanted scholar. She had missed out on a substantial fee when somebody else ran off with her study about the favelas in Rio and used that study for a popular book and film. *Cidade de Deus* went all across the world, and the revenues matched its furore, but not for Alba. "That's what you get when you want to be a scholar", I had said in jest, to which she had responded with a wry smile.

Later that day Alba, Pela and I met as a small group. After the schoolboy's uneasiness and Pela's initial ignoring, the ice was broken. There were no impediments to further interaction. Despite her relatively young age Pela had so far had an eventful life. She had worked as a radio presenter for Jamaican television, got entangled in politics, and had a brother serving in the American army, who had been injured in the war in Iraq. She was currently working on promotion research into civil society and organized crime in Kingston, the capital of Jamaica. Criminal gangs in Kingston's garrisons and Jamaican civil society's responses were her central topic. For research purposes she had conducted interviews in those garrisons—favelas, ghettoes, neighbourhoods—and she had studied how the police force and the army tried to gain control.

It had required courage and nearly everybody had advised her against doing it. Still she had persisted. Like a British-Nigerian researcher, whom I had met some time before and who, in spite of her frail and tender frame, had done fieldwork amidst warring parties in Sierra Leone. Sometimes it seems as if only women have the guts to conduct this type of dangerous fieldwork, perhaps because, strangely enough, they feel less vulnerable amidst warriors and gangstas. Despite the accounts of rape in violent conflicts, it is mostly men who lose their lives. In battle and violent conflict men are usually the perpetrators and victims at the same time.

My keen and sincere interest in Pela's work, and her unembarassed singing and pronunciation of Dutch words in Shanghai's major book store brought us closer together. I had shown her a Chinese-Dutch dictionary, and without fail she started pronouncing the Dutch words aloud. Much to my surprise, this was done with little foreign accent. She had not needed a score for her singing in the bookstore, which the Chinese customers did not even seem to notice, immersed as they were in their reading.

Later after the conference, after she had returned to New Zealand and I in the Netherlands, the connection proved strong enough to be continued at such a distance. Pela sent a number of chapters from her thesis in the making and asked my opinion. Again my interest was raised, which I fervently communicated to her. It was fantastic work, which required courage to write. She was a talented writer as well. In one of the chapters she drew a comparison with the Italian Mafia, although her image and references of the situation in Italy were somewhat dated, in my opinion. Since the early 1990s—when the Mafia was having its heyday—the situation had improved. Naturally, the Mafia had not left Italy altogether, but some 4,000 gang Mafioso, including kingpins, had been put behind bars. Thanks to the EU for its financial and legal efforts, and thanks to the women—either from Mafia or non-Mafia families—who were fed up with violence, proclaiming that enough was enough: *basta e basta*!

I offered to do literature research into more recent events and pointed at the significance these developments in Europe could have for crime-fighting in Jamaica. If Jamaican Dons and Italian Godfathers had something in common, then it was not inconceivable that, just like in Italy, destiny could also be reversible in Jamaica. There could be an end to crude, criminal violence in society, however hopeless the situation may appear to be. That was the message of an article we then wrote together via email, to be published in an academic journal. It was the message of hope, which Pela believed in just as much as I did.

In the meantime she had received a doctorate and was in search of a job, which she finally found in Australia, and later in America. In between she had lived in her own country for a while, where not everything had been easy for her. Of course, it is true there is much partying and making music, and the athletes are a class of their own, but the violence in everyday society had not stopped, despite our article . . .

This was a matter of concern to her, and especially the fact that ordinary people in the street often know exactly who are the criminals, but dare not tell the authorities was the essence of the problem, in her eyes. She had coined a term for it: *informer phobia*, i.e. the fear of people to report criminals, or to use more negative words, the fear of grassing on others. There was sufficient reason for such fears; even in Jamaican pop music there are continuous and undisguised warnings: who talks, dies. I recognized her analysis from accounts about the Mafia, but also from the situation in Afghanistan, where I had done fieldwork a number of times. Now and in the past, Afghan ISAF personnel are threatened in so-called *night letters* that are inconspicuously distributed in the neighborhoods and villages when—after sunglow—life has come to a stop. More often than not, they are simply murdered. That is because they collaborate with the enemy.

The comparison of the violence problem in the two countries—however different—struck us, and we decided to devote another article to the issue. The article comprised theoretical considerations, more comparisons with, for example, the former German Democratic Republic, and recommendations in order to be able to put a stop to this criminal disorder. Pela wrote the epilogue, in which she referred to the importance of courage in these kinds of situations. "After all, one cannot kill all the people that dare to speak", is what she wrote—desperately or resolutely?—in the concluding sentence. With mixed feelings I took notice of this sentence, but abstained from suggesting to changing it. It did leave me a slight sense of despondency, though.

It presumably had the same effect on Pela, when she was back in Jamaica. Her patience was running out. Academic writing yielded little impact in society, she must have thought. This prompted her to write two large articles about this subject for the most prominent newspaper of the country, the *Jamaican Gleaner*. In her previous career as a journalist she had published more often in it. When the two texts—naturally emphasizing the situation in Jamaica—had been published, one shortly after the other, she told me about it and said that for the first time in my life I had published in this authoritative Jamaican newspaper. She had signed the articles with our two names. I was quite taken by the idea, but also a bit surprised. Certainly, all the brainwork had been done together, but the contents were mainly about Jamaica, which was not my contribution. Although for me personally the reference to my name could have been dispensed with, for Pela stressing our joint work had been important. She cherished our friendship and collaboration.

Sometime later I was rather absent-mindedly scrolling through Google, when—lo and behold!—my name suddenly flashed past on a website on Jamaican gangstas. It contained extensive references to the phenomenon of informer phobia, which Pela and I had analysed. The website spoke of extremely interesting findings; rarely had the academic world produced anything as useful as our analysis. I would have preferred not to have seen this at all. "Fortunately, there is a vast ocean between the island and the Netherlands", I could not help thinking. Could informer phobia turn into researcher phobia? I wondered.

LANDING AT SEA

"What is that there at sea you see in the distance?", my younger son asks me. He is pointing at something that had also caught my eye. We are on the beach in the Greek island of Corfu and in the distance there is a colossal structure quivering in the heat. "I do not know, perhaps it is a drilling platform?" While I am saying that I realize it cannot be that. It does not look like a one. "I guess it is a giant ship, but then of a very strange type". We leave it at that, and we pursue our leisure activities, being lazy and going for a swim every now and then. What you cannot know, you must not want to know.

Later in the day we are strolling through the capital of the island, Kerkyra. Among the many tourists we spot groups of American naval personnel and we suppose part of the Sixth Fleet must be moored in the harbour. At the time of the Cold War the Sixth Fleet had orders to follow advancing movements of the Russians in the Mediterranean. When the Russian fleet entered the Mediterranean—"our sea", as the Romans called it—it passed through the Bosporus, not very far from here. We understand, but the connection with the oil-drilling platform we saw earlier that day is still impossible to make.

The connection becomes clear when we see a poster somewhere, which announces that the US aircraft carrier Eisenhower is in the neighbourhood and can be visited by the public on Sunday. The Americans understand that they must show some signs of goodwill to the Greek population, which has a reputation for having communist sympathies. In order to gain some support among the Greeks, the American Navy organizes this 'open day at sea'. From ten o'clock in the morning people that are interested can report at the docks, from where they are ferried to the aircraft carrier every

73

half hour. Reading the announcement has roused my enthusiasm. Some time before that, I had joined the military as a civilian, and that is why I am also professionally interested. "Shall we do that on Sunday?" Only now do I realize what my son and I saw at sea in the distance. The penny has dropped.

Not everyone joins us that Sunday. A couple of people in our small group are totally opposed to violence, and they are therefore also not fond of military objects . . . Others are bent on going on this free outing. The American Navy has organized it well . . . there is continuous ferry that covers the five-kilometre distance to the carrier and back in good time. A stairs at the stern of the iron monster gives us access to the ship. The simple fact that this mass, this rock in the sea, is able to float is hard to imagine.

The first thing we see when we reach the top of the steps is the enormous take-off and landing strip. An aircraft carrier is in fact a large floating airfield, with huge storage and maintenance areas, and accommodation for the personnel. At this ship 4,000 people live and work, a village in itself. They must be fed, their clothes must be washed, people must be able to relax and entertain themselves when not on duty or sleeping. So much of what happens in a military organization is tuned to taking care of the people that may have to go into action.

We first get a tour of the upper deck, the huge take-off and landing area. Here and there aircraft are dispersed on either side. It is remarkable that in reality they look less spectacular than they do in the commercials that are shown worldwide. It is definitely not Top Gun we are looking at; the aircraft make an agonizingly ramshackle impression. There is much rust on the fuselage, due to the salty sea wind, according to our guide, a senior sergeant with a lot of service experience.

Although the space of the take-off and landing strip seems enormous, the parking of the aircraft close to the edge shows how limited the actual space on the main deck really is. Every centimetre counts, it appears. The guide explains how much everyone depends on each other because of the cramped space at the carrier. Everyone, regardless of rank or position, must keep a close watch on each other.

"When they park their aircraft, pilots, the ship's heroes, completely depend on the youngest sailors, the 'deck apes' or 'deck monkeys', the least trained and educated of the crewmembers. To save space the pilots must park their jets as efficiently as possible, during which manoeuvres their cockpits may lean over the edge of the deck. The nose wheel then comes close to the edge, which the pilots are unable to see as the cockpit is in front of the nose wheel. The pilots then only see the waves—pitch black at night—below them. At that moment they are in mortal danger, for if the nose wheel slips one inch further, aircraft and pilot tumble straight into the sea . . . To prevent that from happening the pilots have to have complete faith in the taxi directors who, waving their arms, indicate how far the pilots can advance. "Another five inches . . . . two . . . and one more.", are the instructions given above the turbulent waves. "Here, there are no heroes without assistants . . . and sometimes the assistants are more important. One cannot do without the other, and vice versa".

We listen with fascination, and we try to imagine the fighter pilot's fears when parking the aircraft—a goalkeeper's fear before a penalty, only much more intense. From over the edge I look down, and ten metres below me I can only see masses of dark blue water . . . I think our guide has exaggerated nothing . . . this is really frightening. Manoeuvering fighter jets instills fear, in more ways than one can imagine.

We proceed with our tour of the ship and understand that even the smallest object—a lost bolt—may cause a major disaster. "Most positions on this deck were bought in blood", "Think safety first" and "Safety never takes a break" are just a few of the standard sayings aboard this ship. A bolt may be sucked into a jet engine, and the whole *shebang* will explode. That is also why everyone keeps a keen eye on each other. Each individual's activities are connected with somebody else's. On an aircraft carrier you are never alone, never unobserved, for your own safety and that of others.

We descend into the hull of the ship. The elevators to the hangars and maintenance areas are all idle on a Sunday but, in contrast, there is bustling activity in the kitchen. Even on a Sunday,

4,000 bellies have to be filled three times a day by many busy bees of different colours, ranging from black to yellow to white. White is the predominant colour in the world of pilots, but the rest of the ship's personnel has all the colours in the rainbow. There is effortless cooperation on the ship and everyone mingles with everybody else. When I ask questions about it, they say it is not a big deal, which soon becomes clear.

Our guide believes this integration is self-evident in the US Navy. Since World War II racial integration in the armed forces has developed much further than in any other American company or community. Nowhere are there in American organizations so many non-whites in leading positions, the sergeant—a white serviceman himself—states not entirely without pride.

I talk to a young Afro-American sailor, dressed in white, sweating profusely over a steaming kettle of boiling potatoes. What does he think of working here and can he get along with his colleagues? "Man, it's hot here, you see . . . but we're one team in this place . . . so who cares about white and black! Everyone is fully connected, no matter what colour. Respect man, all over . . . !" Here rules a collective mind, not a racial divide.

His name is Jerry and he is from Detroit. He tells about his family back home, how he got into the navy, and about the young wife he married just before sailing again. A job in the kitchen of USS Eisenhower appealed to him, because there were very few jobs available in Detroit, where the car industry is only shedding jobs. This is a familiar story, the story of so many Americans.

We must move on. There is not much time left for this group of visitors. Other groups are waiting. As we are leaving Jerry calls after us. "Believe me, man . . . racial relations are much better in the armed forces than in civilian life." We would love to believe that. The visit is coming to an end. We have seen enough by now, the enthusiasm of many for technology and weapon systems we do not share. We are ferried back to the beach where we meet the rest of our group . . . and spend another afternoon in the heat of the Grecian sun, in the distance that 'funny oil-drilling island'.

In the evening we take what has become our customary walk into town looking for an outdoor cafe. It is another hot summer night, and there is much to see and do. In the little harbour we see one of the cutters of USS Eisenhower with a score of sailors on board, on leave for the evening. They no longer look like sailors; they are now wearing the uniform of the average tourist. In contrast to what we saw on board, there is separation on the basis of the colour of skin. The whites are seated to one side, the blacks to the other. When the sloop arrives this pattern continues; the whites go to the right, the blacks to the left. It is very clear they will only see each other again when they paddle back to the Eisenhower later that night.

I see Jerry in the latter group and I warmly greet him. We pat each other on the shoulder, but I immediately ask him about this segregation. He laughs heartily, "I told you, man . . . race relations are much better in the armed forces than in civilian life!"

Now I understand, again somewhat belated. 'Racial integration' stops immediately when you leave the ship; it only applies when you are at work on board. Going ashore in Kerkyra is 'civilian life', and then you want to be amongst friends . . .

Madame Butterfly

In an insignificantly little car, painted in a military green colour, we drive past the monument of Sun Yat-sen, the national father of all Chinese people. Mats, my Swedish colleague and I are in Taipei, the capital of Taiwan, the unrecognized state with 23 million Chinese inhabitants situated off the coast of mainland China. We have just had a rendez-vous with the Under-Secretary for Defence to discuss the research plan of an international study into the consequences of the abolition of conscription. The Swedes are currently going through the same process. That is the reason for this Swedish-Taiwanese connection, in which I act as intermediary.

In Sweden the abolition of national service is hardly an issue, as so many European countries have led the way to a professional volunteer army. In Taiwan, however, it is a very delicate subject. A volunteer army is always smaller than a conscript army, while mainland China has no immediate intention to abolish conscription soon. If necessary, that country could call up millions of soldiers, which is a horrific notion to the Under-Secretary.

But other appointments were waiting for him, so we have some time on our hands to see something of the city. We are accompanied by Major Lydia Lee, who, on being asked, avows not to be a hard-core soldier. Originally she is an opera singer, a mezzo-soprano. She had done a few performances in the National Theatre, but that yielded too little fame and certainty. That is why she is a major in the Taiwanese army now, whose assignment today is to accompany foreign visitors. As an educated opera singer she has mastered the main European languages, which explains her assignment.

She tells us that there are few leading parts for mezzo-sopranos, Carmen being the only exception of importance. Carmen? This is my favourite opera! Immediately I start singing the *Habanera*, and after some hesitation, she joins in, more quietly, more modestly, and far better, of course. After that the various other popular parts of that opera are reviewed. We are enjoying ourselves, and Mats informs us that he a talented whistler, which we shall hear more of in the days to come.

When we have done the entire repertoire from Carmen, I ask her to sing the final aria from Madame Butterfly. Surely she knows it, when you think of opera in Asia. But she does not know the piece from memory, and she is not supposed to know it, because the main part in that opera is for a soprano, and not for a mezzo, she says hesitantly. Apparently that difference plays an important role in study and career opportunities.

It does not take her long to find the romantic tragedy of Madame Butterfly on her smartphone: the Japanese woman, who commits suicide, because she is left by her American naval officer and father of her child, after she had also been cast out by her own family. She should have known better to have married that foreigner . . . The dramatic climax is the arrival of her American naval officer's new wife, who has come to claim the child . . . hér child . . . The dramatic final aria of *Povera Butterfly*—oh, poor butterfly—sounds a bit thin through the smartphone . . . Lydia nor I can sing along.

Two days later we are guests at the Defence Academy of Japan. Our colleague there, Taro Yamamoto, will participate in the research, just like our colleagues from Belgium, France, Turkey, Poland and Swiss. Germany does not take part. 'There is no time' our German colleagues are made to say on their bosses' orders. The real reason, however, may very well be that the abolition of conscription is currently too hot a potato in Chancellor Merkel's Germany, and they do not want anybody prying.

Taro's reception in a traditional restaurant is fantastic. The eight courses, with the sake and Asahi beers, are more than we had dared to expect. But the place is also steeped in history: "This restaurant finds itself in one of the few buildings south of Tokyo that survived the Second World War." What came to be known as the Tokyo Fire Raid of March 1945 consumed everything in a blazing heat. It will not be the last time that the war features in one of the conversations. In order to try and relax the atmosphere a bit I mention our meeting with the opera singer in Taiwan, and Madame Butterfly, the opera that plays in the land of the rising sun.

He knows the story, but quickly adds that something similar could never happen nowadays. "Japanese women of today are emancipated, free, and independent . . . and when they marry foreigners they often exert great influence." "Great influence, Taro?" "Well yes, what do you think of Yoko Ono, she drove the Beatles apart, did not she . . . ? A real bitch, something entirely different from a poor butterfly . . ." Some days later and after some more thinking and research, he produces two more names: Komito Goto, former French race driver Jean Alesi's wife, and Dewi Sukarno currently living in Tokyo, known in the Netherlands because her husband freed Indonesia from that European colonizer. Taro is preoccupied with banning the image of the dependent and castaway Japanese woman. What he means to say is that the Japanese woman is not to be looked upon a poor butterfly anymore.

The next day, after Mats and I have given a seminar on international military cooperation, Taro takes us to the US Naval Base at Yokohama, for having a beer and a decent hamburger. In this town thousands of sailors live in naval barracks. Thousands more come here for relaxation, when the 7th Fleet arrives to be resupplied and to be inspected. The aircraft carriers and the submarines have nuclear propulsion, and nuclear fuel is dangerous. Nothing should go wrong there, as some Americans in the officers' mess readily agree to. They are non-military hired civilians, who check the welding of the pipes on board. Critical and dangerous work, I conclude and they confirm.

Tomorrow it is back to the grind again for them and I wonder if the same restriction applies to them as to pilots: no alcohol on the day before work. "Yeah man . . . you are probably right, but as long as we are in 75% shape, things will be fine . . . and there are so many protocols . . . things cannot go wrong." These men are just too amiable to be found fault with for what they say. We order another round of beers.

After the beers Taro, Mats and I feast on our hamburgers. I enquire about the so-called international relations between Japanese (and other Asian) women and American naval personnel. These relations are numerous, Taro agrees, but it is not always plain sailing. In the past there was sexual misconduct in the bars and out on the street, but that is something the American naval command keeps a close eye on nowadays. The number of divorces in international marriages is very high according to Japanese standards, but not to American ones. More than once there is hackling about the children after a divorce, but there are no Madame Butterfly dynamics, Taro hastens to add.

On our one-kilometre walk back to the hotel we bump into eight ferociously looking US Navy military police constables, seven male and one female.

On the twelfth floor of the hotel I inspect the escape routes. Taro has told us that there is always the danger of earthquakes in Japan. "Even now", he had added with a smile, at the same time reassuring us that, "our construction engineers know how to build. Our flat buildings are built on shock absorbers." After some searching I have found the stairs going down and I hope I can get down swiftly enough when the building starts shaking. I do not give it too much thought; I trust the Japanese engineers and their shock absorbers.

The next day we have an appointment with the director of the officers' courses at the academy, a Japanese air force general. We discuss the strategic situation in the Pacific with him in the light of our research into the abolition of conscription in Sweden and Taiwan, a change of policy mainland China is not yet contemplating. On this journey we have heard a number of times that China is bent on maintaining a large conscript army. Japan, on the other hand, ended conscription immediately after the war, under the pressure of international politics.

In the Japanese army China is none too popular. My enthusiastic account of a young female Chinese colleague at my university in the Netherlands with qualifications from Beijing University brings about an icy-cold silence across the table. Apparently my manner was too enthusiastic, saying she was so intelligent, so nice . . . Taro later discloses that not so long ago a Japanese defence attache was arrested for falling in love with a Chinese lady, who turned out to be a spy, which is referred to as being 'honey-trapped'.

The slowly dissipating silence proves how delicate a matter this is. The Japanese military leadership is concerned about the activities of mainland China, which is just about to raise its defence budget with another 13%. Such a growth percentage cannot be matched by any other country, not even by the Americans. The Japanese do not really trust the Americans anymore and the relation with that huge country has become ambivalent. Hatred and affection struggle for supremacy in the hearts of the Japanese people.

The suffering of the war has not yet fully worn off. The atom bombs should never have fallen, in the eyes of the Japanese. Japan had already been vanquished by the Tokyo Fire Raid. The bombs with their radioactive radiation, which later generations of Japanese still have in their bones and glands, were no more than a form of retaliation for Pearl Harbor. Of course, it was also a signal to the former Soviet Union to show how strong the Americans were. And perhaps it was also an experiment to find out how vast the destructive power of this brand new technology really was. It was an experiment that took place over the heads of generations of Japanese, our conversation partners add hesitantly. We wisely do not talk about the massacre of Nanjing, the Burmese railway line and the blood of Iwo Jima, as it is best left unmentioned.

In contrast, the Americans are also liked in Japan. The presence of their 7th Fleet keeps the Chinese at bay, and that is vital. Japan consists of a number of large islands and a whole string of smaller ones, stretching from north to south, from the Russian to the Chinese coast. Japan is engaged in disputes with these superpowers about some of these islands, which occasionally leads to real military skirmishes. That worries the Japanese military. Particularly the Senkaka islands close to Taiwan, and therefore also to mainland China, give rise to concern: there are ever-increasing confrontations in the East China Sea off the coast of these islands. Japan claims these islands on historical grounds; the Chinese claim them because they are right in front of their shores.

I ask the general why it would be so bad if the Chinese took possession of these small islands. I know that for China it is important to have easy access to the Pacific Ocean. I also know the sensitivity of these matters by now, so I quickly add, in an effort not to appear foolish, that the question is a mere theoretical one. The small islands are almost uninhabited, there is some fishing, but the ocean is vast and the possible presence of minerals is yet to be proven.

The general looks at me as if I have gone insane. "That would be totally against the soul of Japan", he stammers. The thought that they could also sell the small islands at a handsome price I wisely keep to myself. Probably better to spend thousands of millions on the extension of the fleet and air force than receive billions in the sale of these sparsely inhabited islets. The military mind almost always works like that.

The Japanese do not really dare to have complete faith in the Americans anymore. Their economic power is dwindling, and America has already stacked enough weight on its shoulders as it is. Besides, America will think twice before it takes action against the huge economic superpower, China. America's economy would be torn to shreds, and just wait and see: soon Europe will be selling arms to China. Europe will just have to, because there will not be any other way to earn sufficient money. That is why Japan will have to learn to stand on its own two legs, for better or for worse. Japan is afraid to be left alone: an elderly lady without her make-up, discarded . . .

On our flight back we fly around the conical shape of Mount Fuji for an hour. The volcanic mountain towers above the clouds and finds itself between heaven and earth. Impressive.

Five days later an earthquake and tsunami strike Japan. There is huge devastation on land, the fires cause a diabolical heat, and once again there is the threat of a nuclear disaster. *Povera Giappone.*

"Unskilled and unaware of it"

When Dutch armed forces were deployed to Uruzgan in 2006, it was clear that this would be one of the most difficult missions since the Korean War. In their effort to control Afghanistan the Soviets had hardly ventured into that province, which was the cradle of the Taliban. The Netherlands was the only non-Anglo-Saxon country to send troops in a leading role to the dangerous South, bordering on Pakistan. Other troop-contributing countries were Canada, Australia, and, of course, America and Britain.

It would be an operation against insurgents and terrorists, formidable opponents with whom the Dutch had little experience. But Britain had, at least that is what could be heard all around. British generals and colonels told everyone that the situation in Southern Afghanistan would be similar to Northern Ireland. In Bosnia they had said the same. A colleague of mine told me that a British Brigadier had told him this repeatedly when, as a young lieutenant colonel, he served under him in Sarajevo. "Have a good look at how we do things. We have had thirty years of operational experience in Belfast and Londonderry." I have heard Swedish and American officers echo this mantra on various occasions.

Intellectuals from the famous think tank in London also chipped in with a quasi-scientific observation, "Northern Ireland took us forty years, so Afghanistan will take us another forty years". Invariably, the use of the word 'so' indicates a thinking error. In this case perhaps two or three errors were made. Nevertheless, this remark was almost triumphantly made for everyone to hear during academic conferences, which is ample reason for digging into Northern Ireland's history of the last half century.

Just like grammar school pupils going on excursions to Rome, prospective officers go on battlefield tours during their training course. Considering the nature of present-day conflicts, a visit to Waterloo is not as relevant as a visit to Kosovo or Northern Ireland. I find Kosovo interesting, but Northern Ireland even more, especially because of the connection made with the military activities in Southern Afghanistan. A visit to that area sheds light on how well the conflict between Protestants and Catholics has been 'managed', and still is today, because years after the cease-fire the conflict still has not been solved. A few days before we depart to Northern Ireland, a police constable was killed in a bomb attack, and the police foiled a second attempt. It does resemble Afghanistan! What was intended to be a journey into history has all of a sudden become current news. Our touring party is given the official instruction to keep a low profile. No uniforms, and certain establishments in Belfast—mentioned by name—must be avoided.

There have not been problems between Protestants and Catholics anywhere in the world for centuries. Tensions, small tensions perhaps, but no major problems, let alone violent ones. In conflicts between the two Christian religions in Northern Ireland almost 4,000 people have lost their lives over the last thirty years. Over 50,000 were wounded, often permanently disabled. From a military perspective, tens of thousands of British soldiers have gained operational experience in this miniature area, the last remnant of Britain on Irish soil, the size of one of the larger Dutch provinces.

This is what British military people and academics pride themselves on, but with what justification? Even if you allow your imagination to run away with you, you would not be able to imagine such a conflict emerging in the Netherlands. Why did Northern Ireland go mad? Where did it go wrong?

At the office of Northern Ireland Affairs of the British Government—our first stop—a female civil servant tells us on being asked that it has become clear by now that a purely military approach to this kind of conflict does not work. A male colleague adds that the first few years of the conflict were primarily a period of "missed opportunities".

In Belfast we are offered two tours, one under the supervision of a guide from the Catholic camp, the other by a Protestant guide. Very soon either of them makes clear that this conflict is not about religion at all. Paddy, the Catholic guide, says resolutely, "God and I parted years ago". Later on we are told that religion serves as a smoke screen. Paddy insists on being a Republican, who wants the tiny northern part of the island to be part of the Irish Republic. That Northern Ireland is still part of Britain is nothing short of colonialism. The more radical elements in his party speak of 'occupied territory'. Paddy himself has become older, sadder, and wiser, which is not surprising after having been in British captivity for years on end. These days he wears a jacket with a 'Peace & Reconciliation' badge, sponsored by the European Union.

We walk through the area where there was so much misery in 1969 and following years, the concrete jungle of Shankill Road and Falls Road. First we go through the Catholic part, where Bombay Street was once set fire to. We halt at the monument for the fallen and are astounded when we see the cages built around the back gardens of the houses. Even projectiles that are pelted over a wall as high as the 'peace wall' land in these gardens, which explains the lattice work, and which is obviously still necessary. The peace is brittle.

Then we pass Divis high-rise flat. In the two upper floors British soldiers took up positions to have a clear view of the town below. "At the same time the inhabitants of the flats on the lower floors acted as a human shield against IRA attacks, just like Khadaffi does in his own country at the moment", Paddy adds quietly, but meaningfully.

In the meantime it has started to rain so heavily that we decide to buy an umbrella. In a grocer's shop we are glad to find one: some time later we discover that green is the dominant colour of the umbrellas, the colour of the Irish Republic. When we pass the iron gates that mark the boundary between the Catholic and Protestant parts, Nigel and I look each other in the eye. "Now the Protestants must be thinking that we belong to Sinn Fein . . . that would not be good!" we say, suppressing a nervous grin, both aware that in these streets many people lost their lives.

Another uneasy moment presents itself when, in all my naïvity, I ask our Protestant guide why he was in prison all those years. Like Paddy, he has made no secret about his years of detention. He is proud of it, but my question is of a different nature. An uneasy silence follows; there is tension in the air. Then he laughs and says, "Because they c'ght me . . ." I do not hear what he says and—still exceedingly naïve—urge him to repeat it. After three efforts I understand: "Because they caught me". As he walks on he adds, "That's why", pointing his prodding finger like the barrel of a pistol into my direction as he speaks.

The next station is Derry, or Londonderry, whichever you prefer. This small town declared itself a 'safe area' at the end of the 1960s. A relic of that time can still be seen in the streets: 'YOU ARE NOW ENTERING FREE DERRY'. It was the time of worldwide student protest, in Paris, Berkeley, or Amsterdam, the years of civil right movements, such as the Black Panthers, who wanted to make clear to the world they had quite a lot to fight for.

Although religion no longer seems to be an issue in Northern Ireland, in those days it was . . . , in any case it caused a divide between two social groupings with unequal opportunities. In Derry or Londonderry—the former preferred by Catholics, who favour the union with Ireland, the latter used by Protestants, who want to remain British—the dividing lines can still be seen. On top of the hill there are the houses of the people, who came from England and settled here centuries ago, down below you find the workers' houses of the Catholic population. Nowadays the differences are less poignant, but photographs of these bygone times still show how wide the gap in living conditions must have been.

In accordance with the spirit of the time civil rights movements started among the Catholic population of Northern Ireland, which held demonstrations against the discrimination of Catholics in terms of politics, housing, and employment. Protestant groups responded, at the same time provoking the Catholics, with the notorious Orange marches, which gradually made the situation increasingly violent.

This resulted in an unstoppable vicious circle of violence, counter-violence, and new violence. Barricades in the streets, stones, bottles, bombs, and then forced house-moving. Everyone had to go to his or her 'own' neighbourhood. Northern Ireland became a war zone. After allowing matters to take their course in political, social, and economic respect, the British Government came into action and decided in 1969 to send the army as peacekeepers.

At first all went well, when British soldiers were welcomed by the population, certainly also by the Catholic community, who gave them tea and cookies. That image deteriorated rather quickly. In the eyes of many the British army turned from friend to enemy. In Northern Ireland people were not used to barbed wire, curfews, batons, teargas, and even bayonets fixed on rifles, and certainly not to arresting men in the street and locking them up without being tried, and breaking into houses with sledgehammers searching for weapons, the so-called 'hard knocks'. The agonizing finale was Sunday, Bloody Sunday in January 1972.

In the Free Derry Museum we meet with John Kelly. His brother Michael—then 17—was one of the fourteen casualties shot dead by British paratroopers on that fateful day. John Kelly is the personification of politeness and dignity. He restrains his emotions about what happened, allowing the museum to express the message for him. He is different from the other people we meet in that he never refers to the British soldiers as 'rottweilers' or 'killing machines'. He is convinced that justice will prevail, and that is what it looks like. 2010 saw the completion of a new, large-scale, official investigation into what happened on that fatal Sunday.

One of the conclusions is that the victims were innocent and unarmed and that in previous inquiries false witness statements were made. Following the outcome of the investigation into the 'unjustified and unjustifiable' conduct of British troops at the time, the current British Government has apologized. This finally enables those concerned to start legal proceedings, which is expected to take place before too long. In the meantime the murals, the huge wall paintings, keep emotions very much alive.

At the end of our journey, during a seminar organized especially for us, Irish junior officers and a British historian give their opinion about the actions of the British army in the first few years. Theirs is an unrelenting judgment.

The British army adhered too much to the recipe it had used for the colonial warfare in Aden, Kenya, and Malaya, with the employment of harsh means and too little eye for the local 'hearts and minds'. Banners with instructions in Arab, as they had been used in Aden, were hung up in the streets of Northern Ireland, showing how much the British army was still occupied with the previous war. There was also too much dependence on one local party—also on the basis of a colonial recipe—in this case the Loyalists with their paramilitary units. In deciding what regiments would be deployed in the Province, the (un)voiced preferences of some military units were too little taken into account. The Black Watch from the Protestant part of Scotland and the Parachute Regiment involved in Bloody Sunday were clear examples of a mismatch. It happened under the watchful eyes of cameras that had been absent in Kenya and Malaya.

On being asked during the coffee break about the relevance of the British experiences for the operations in Afghanistan, my conversation partner from the Irish army is quite clear. "The British army has learnt a lot from the first few years, operations have improved since then and have become more restrained, but after these tragic first few years everything was just a matter of too little, too late . . . the damage was done, the early shootings triggered decades of violence. Soon after deployment the British army became part of the problem. In the eyes of the radicals it became the enemy that had to be killed. And so it happened."

"Understandably, when they were under constant fire and constantly suffered casualties themselves, the British soldiers, in return, could only see the Northern Irish and IRA radicals as enemies, bandits and urban warriors. It became war . . . war . . . war . . . for all parties, lasting for more than thirty years. Only when it dawned on all parties that this war could not be won by anybody, was there room for political and social solutions . . ."

Rather late in the day, this discovery, I thought to myself, but I did not utter a word. My conversation partner continues, "The entire process is comparable with the good intentions of soldiers that want to neutralize one terrorist, but with a direct hit kill almost fifty people and wound more than a hundred during an Afghan wedding, which happened in the summer of 2002. These kinds of occurrences drive people insane. This is how one creates one's enemies . . . for years to come . . . for decades. The dead do not come to life again, but their memory lives on. As a result it only gets worse instead of better . . . it is entirely counter-productive . . . it cannot be mended . . ."

I am left wondering about the question why so many recommend the approach in Northern Ireland as a recipe for operations in Afghanistan . . . Is it collective self-deceit? Doing something badly is bad enough. Doing something badly, and thinking and saying you are doing the right thing, is infinitely worse. The recommendation to apply the British approach in Ulster to the operations in Afghanistan is like advising a patient with lung cancer to smoke a package of cigarettes each and every day . . .

Ignorance is bliss.

On our last night we are taken out to the Temple Bar in Dublin. There are two lady singers only performing songs from women vocalists. People in the crowd, ecstatic from the beer, but also from themselves, sing along with well-known tunes from Alanis Morissette, Tammy Wynette, and the Mamas from the Papas. Women's songs, how appropriate! Women around the world play an important role in reconciliation and the cessation of violence. In pre-war Chicago women put an end to corruption and violence, for which one of them received the Nobel Prize for Peace. Women have largely curbed the influence of the Mafia in Sicily. In Liberia a woman transformed warlords into ordinary men again, and she also got the Noble Peace Prize for it. Women show much more wisdom in these matters, at least most of them do . . .

Stevie Nicks also comes along and makes her self heard, *"Don't stop thinking about tomorrow, yesterday's gone . . . oh, yesterday's go . . . ho . . . hone . . ."*

REVIEW AND RESPONSIBILITY

REVIEW AND RESPONSIBILITY

This collection of stories originates from an idea of a journalist of a leading Dutch newspaper, 'De Volkskrant', Noel van Bemmel, who in 2006 made an appeal to Dutch soldiers with experience in Afghanistan to take those experiences down in writing. Certainly in the Dutch language there is no tradition among military personnel to entrust their experiences to a large audience. In contrast with Britain and America, which have a 'military' writing tradition, the Netherlands armed forces and its activities are not so popular with the Dutch population. So, what is the use of writing anything down?

However, the appeal has had ample response, resulting in the book 'Task Force Uruzgan', which was first published in 2009. Already in the first round I had reported myself to 'De Volkskrant': I could write something about my brush with fear during one of my visits to Kabul. I had been there twice as employee—civilian employee—of the Netherlands Defence Academy.

The editorial staff at 'De Volkskrant' thought this was interesting, because servicemen do not normally tell much about the fears they may have had during their mission. But I was not a serviceman. Anyway, nothing came of it. I was too busy, and perhaps it was not that important what I had to say. A year later—stuck to the sofa with an injury from an unhappy fall from my bike—I was contacted by 'De Volkskrant' again. There was to be a new edition of the book shortly, and there was room for a couple of new stories, so would I still be interested? I had enough time on my hands, so I set to work. The fruit of my labours is the first chapter of this book, which was also included in the fifth edition of Task Force Uruzgan.[1]

I was beginning to enjoy writing such stories. Over the past few years I had made many trips to do research during military missions of UN and NATO. I thought going there myself was a better approach, and more interesting, than sending the usual questionnaires that are so dominant in present-day social-scientific research. Most of the fieldresearch was done under the auspices of the Dutch Ministry of Defence, but a few times it was on invitation and under the authority of the Belgian, Swedish and Canadian armed forces.

There was always a lot to tell about these trips, but what I had committed to paper was limited to academic treatises. That was the purpose of fieldwork: to scrutinize certain aspects of military missions. At first this entailed the multinational cooperation between the soldiers of the various countries, but gradually also encompassed questions about the effectiveness of the activities in areas of operations. By degrees I combined the two fields of interest into research about the working of the various national operational styles and methods of conflict resolution. I had also participated in routine working visits to mission areas and the odd study trip, which had already been organized anyway. Occasionally, I had been involved in counselling on the organization of officers' training courses, even as far afield as Bolivia.

My position was always that of the relative outsider. I was in the military, and occasionally I wore uniform only when I had to, but it was unreal. My presence in mission areas was too short to really become one with the men and women at the camp. Such a position has advantages and disadvantages: it implies that you have to steer a middle course between involvement and distance, as the renowned sociologist Norbert Elias once put it. These collected stories clearly show the strength and weakness of this position.

The stories also reveal how much one's own perceptions and associations play a role in what one experiences. Often I saw things my travel companions had overlooked; perhaps sometimes I observed things that were never really there. The imagination can play tricks on you, and most of the time you do not realize that, or you do not want to know. In these stories I have operated the camera myself, and more importantly, I was responsible for the selection and editing.

So these are my stories, which I have written about what I have experienced, and in this sense the book is more fiction-faction than a factual travel book. People's names have been changed, sometimes persons are composites, small facts may have been distorted slightly, events have been combined or have moved in time, and sometimes quotes have been exaggerated. In some stories—particularly 'Landing at Sea'—other writings were used as a source of inspiration.

Such adaptations are pardonable, because often, perhaps mostly, things are not really what they seem. According to Marukami there is something magical to be found in reality: what you see is not there, and what you do not see, is there.[2] That is, I think, also what these stories try to convey. In any case they are *petites histoires* used to show something of the bigger picture.

Missions and mission areas

The countries that feature in most of the stories are areas in post-conflict situations. At the same time, they are regions where there is a lot of poverty. Afghanistan, Liberia and the Congo are among the poorest countries in the world, where appalling violence has dominated daily life and, unfortunately, still plays a major role. Azerbeidhjan, Benin, Bolivia, Kirgizia—other countries that serve as scenery in my stories—also belong to the bottom billion, the most deprived parts of the world.[3] This summing up shows that violence and poverty against the background of a youthful population go hand in hand. Not always, because in the Lebanon, formerly the 'Pearl of the Middle East', and in Northern Ireland, poverty is not so poignant, and even less in Japan, Taiwan, and China. Yet in these regions national security is not taken for granted, at least not by the people over there.

All in all, the military efforts in these widely divergent regions have very different backgrounds. And these efforts have equally varying levels of success. In order to find out more, I went there to see for myself, which calls for a further explanation for each story.

Matter of fact, but not cynical

This trip I made in January 2009, accompanied by two colleagues. The intention was to do fieldwork for research into the Effects-Based Approach to Operations (EBAO) in Afghanistan, as the system is known within NATO. The idea is that no military operations are actuated without certainty about the desired effect, and without the certainty what can be achieved with a certain action. Follow-up actions can only be started when it is known what has been achieved by a previous action. It introduces a kind of administrative thinking some military are not particularly fond of. We were in Kabul as well as in Kandahar to map out the international command and control at the various levels. Unfortunately we could not proceed on our journey to Uruzgan, the province at that time controlled by the Dutch armed forces, because a major operation was going on.

The work we did during this visit has led to a number of research publications. The main finding was that this subject was a hot topic, and that there is much discussion going on among personnel of the different armed services (Air Force personnel are more in favour than Marines for instance), and that internationally armed forces deal with it in different ways. The connection of data and reports between the different operational levels is far from perfect. In other words, there is room for improvement and further development of this mode of working.

A newspaper article in 'De Volkskrant' of 7 April 2011 proves that the thought of a traffic accident in Kabul with military involvement is not so imaginary. A British army vehicle had killed a female pedestrian and injured another woman and child, as a result of which an angry Afghan crowd threw stones at British soldiers.

A new formula

The fieldwork in the Congo, on which this story is based, took place in November 2009. Two colleagues and I made the initial planning to do research into the multinational control of the largest UN mission (MONUC). At an early stage we found that the mission—despite all UN's good intentions—had, and still has, a huge problem where its reputation and the support for the mission from the country's population and politicians are concerned. This issue was so prominent, certainly in the period that we were there, that it demanded all our attention. It resulted in an informal memorandum with recommendations for UN officials and in a publication about this specific subject in a Canadian volume of articles. A second publication for an American book is in the making.

Meanwhile MONUC has been given another name, MONUSCO, the mandate has been renewed and slightly changed, and some contingents of the UN forces have been withdrawn, as a response to the demands, wishes, and expectations the Congolese politicians had put forward so poignantly in the week of our presence. In the meantime the Congo remains a political hornets' nest and everyday violence against the population continues like never before, especially in the areas where UN presence is limited.

An unexpected low

This event happened when a Belgian colleague and myself were on our way to Afghanistan, where we would be doing research at Kabul military airport in March 2006. It was the intention to gather data for her thesis by doing interviews and making observations about the everyday life (*'la vie quotidienne'*) of Belgian soldiers participating in the ISAF mission. More particularly we were interested in the functioning of Belgian (sub) commanders on the spot. My unfortunate fall into a cellar in Baku interfered with this plan, but before we separated we were able to discuss how we—my Belgian colleague, in fact—could carry out the collection of data. The research approach we agreed upon was successfully put into practice in Kabul and it led to a wonderful publication, which also appeared to be useful for her thesis.

Baptism of fire

Again at the request and under the supervision of the Belgian armed forces the two of us could do fieldwork in an area of operations, this time during the UNIFIL mission in southern Lebanon, just north of the border with Israel. In the 1970s the Netherlands made a considerable contribution to this mission. The Belgian contingent was there—and still is—to run a field hospital and to clear mines in the fields and meadows, which were left behind after the most recent military actions. Both types of activity are humanitarian and are much appreciated by the local population, all the more because local patients can be treated in the Belgian as well as the Chinese field hospital of the mission. It speaks for itself that the population is very glad with the mine-clearing activities. The research, once again focusing on *'la vie quotidienne militaire'*, has resulted in a number of modest publications, and there are probably more to follow. The fieldwork for this research was conducted in January 2008. The account of the events taking place in Rwanda in April 1994 is based on the memoirs of General Dallaire.[4]

The mysterious other person

In October 2006, at the request, and on invitation, of Swedish colleagues I could avail myself of the possibility to do fieldwork into the functioning of the bi-national (Irish-Swedish) Quick Reaction Force of the UNMIL mission in Liberia. The immediate cause was the irritation and lack of understanding on the part of the Swedish military about the functioning of the Irish. It was more of an internal problem, because the functioning of the whole UN mission, which is really rather successful, was not discussed. Nor were the African military colleagues, who did the real work in the streets of Monrovia and elsewhere. In the two publications that evolved on the basis of the fieldwork, this 'inner directedness' of the Swedes has also been identified as a problem. In this story some of my observations have been inspired by the report Zadie Smith wrote about her trip through Liberia.[5]

Slob!

This story has its origin in the same trip that serves as the basis of the first story. Again the background is the military headquarters of the ISAF mission in Kabul and Kandahar in January 2009.

¡El pueblo unido...!

The events in this story took place in September 2004. This time the purpose of my visit was not research, but exchanging experiences with organizing educational programmes for officer training courses. In Bolivia it was 'time for change', which we only fully realized when we were there. The military authorities in the country, traditionally the vestige of European Bolivians, felt that the social pressure on their institutes was growing, which was the reason why the Canadian military academy was asked for advice. The Canadians in turn asked representatives of the British and Dutch institutes for officer training to join them, so they could substantiate their own experiences and advice on the basis of those of others. It was a kind of military development aid, so to speak.

It would take until January 2006 for Evo Morales to be elected the first 'Indigenous President' of Bolivia. Since his inauguration much has changed in the country. Sergio Ortega wrote the Chilean battle song, which provided the title of this story, in 1973 at the time of the Allende government.

A newspaper article in 'De Volkskrant', dating 6 May 2011, features the headline 'Bolivia Demands Open Access to the Sea from Chili', signifying that the tension with neighbouring Chili about a strip of land on the coast of the Pacific Ocean still exists today. I owe the closing sentence to Esmeralda Kleinreesink.

Face protectors

The notion that interpreters are essential in overseas military operations may not be all that evident for everyone, certainly not for American and British military people, who have assumed for a long time that the entire world speaks—or wants to speak—their language. The Dutch know their language is insignificant on a worldwide scale. That is why from time immemorial the Dutch have employed a relatively large number of interpreters, who were aware of the operational impact of their activities.

We started this research plan in November and December 2003 in Bosnia, which we continued in Afghanistan with fieldwork on various occasions and with a range of researchers. The experiences, which are the basis of this story, have led to one academic publication. Later on more was to follow, drawn up by, and in cooperation with, other researchers. Meanwhile the importance of 'language management' in overseas operations has also dawned on the Americans.

The cynical definition of the work of interpreters is from Ambrose Pierce; for part of the dialogues I have allowed myself to be inspired by the Afghan adventures of Rory Stewart.[6] The closing sentence I owe to Andrea van Dijk, and a little to myself.

Fighting Falcons

This story is a compilation of two orientation trips, that is to say, trips without explicit research purposes. One of them was to Villa Franca airbase in Italy, from where, within the framework of operations over the Balkans, Dutch and Belgian F-16s carried out patrols in the mid-1990s. The other trip was an excursion of Dutch Advanced Staff College students to Kirgizia, from where the first aerial operations over Afghanistan were flown. The tasks then were very similar to what Dutch F-16s have been doing in the Libyan airspace in the spring and summer of 2011. These flights were also flown from an Italian airbase.

Superstition and other discomforts

It was once said that "A story ain't a story, if it ain't two stories." This also goes for this story about Belgium and Benin. First and foremost the story is about the young officers from Benin, who have to reintegrate into their own armed forces after finishing their studies in Brussels. This does not necessarily go smoothly and in order to map this out we embarked on this trip. The fieldwork fits well within the framework of the research for the thesis of a colleague in Brussels. At the same time we were made very welcome by the Belgian authorities and personnel in the African country, which led to the writing of this story.

Meanwhile two academic treatises have evolved from this fieldwork, yet to be published. One—in English—deals with the inter-generational dynamics that occur when young, highly-educated officers return to their own armed forces, and one in French, which focuses on the cultural differences between studying in Europe and working in Africa. The fieldwork took place in June 2010.

The Chinese connection

These series of events started in Shanghai in June 2005 and have been unfolding ever since, in exactly the way it has been discussed in the story. The story has not ended yet. The two of us have committed ourselves to writing a book on violence in contemporary societies (working title: Armageddon), using email correspondence only. The British-Nigerian researcher referred to is Funmi Olonisakin, who published a doctorate on her fieldwork in Sierra Leone, where at that time a civil war was raging.

Landing At Sea

The observations underlying this story date back a long time (August 1998) and result from the haphazard course of events it describes. This story borrows extensively from military-sociological and psychological work from American authors, who did research into racial relations in the US Army and the internal relations on board naval vessels, in particular aircraft carriers.[7] The essence of the story—the crucial observation about racial harmony on board during working hours as opposed to race segregation after work—is my own. The way in which I have perceived and established it corresponds with the way in which I have described it.

Madame Butterfly

This story is the fruit of a trip for which a Swedish colleague had invited me. The trip was made in connection with the preparation of an international study into the abolition of conscription in Sweden and Taiwan. The new experiences in these two countries would be compared with those of countries where national service had already become a thing of the past, such as Japan and the Netherlands, and countries like Swiss and Turkey, which still have conscript armies.

Even before my departure I had made up my mind that, if this trip would yield a story, its title would be Madame Butterfly. The tragic theme of Madame Butterfly has been made famous by the opera of Giacomo Puccini (1904), which was based on an American novel written a few years earlier.[8] Right from the starting point the story almost wrote itself. All the events and findings matched with the theme of the opera, beginning with the opera-singer we met in Taipe. This clearly was the magic of reality!

The trip took place late February/early March 2011, a couple of day before the Tsunami devastated large parts of Japan and destroyed nuclear reactors. At home and at work people were relieved that I had managed to get away in the nick of time.

"Unskilled and unaware of it"

This story finds its origin in the experiences I have gathered during a study trip of officer-cadets and midshipmen of the Strategic Studies Department of the Netherlands Defence Academy. We made this trip in April 2011, and although I scarcely give lectures to students of this Department, I was invited to join, for which I am still grateful to my colleagues. Participating in the excursion was important for me, because of a writing project in which I compare the British and Dutch style of operating in the Afghan provinces of Helmand and Uruzgan. To be able to give possible differences a sound basis, I also compare British and Dutch government action at the time of violent internal disruptions, such as during the 'Troubles' in Northern Ireland and the Moluccan actions of the 1970s, respectively. Much can be read about these subjects, but the opportunity to watch matters for one self and to speak with experts on the spot is extremely helpful.

When writing this story I checked a number of data by consulting two authoritative books about the 'Troubles' in Northern Ireland. The story of the tragic Afghan wedding I also borrowed from an existing book.[9] Lord Saville's hefty report on Bloody Sunday can be perused on the Internet.[10] The title of this story comes from a renowned social-psychological research into the excessive self-assurance of very many people. Many of them—more men than women—estimate their own abilities much higher than what they really are or possibly can be.[11]

Words of thanks

I am not a hero when it comes to travelling on my own. Nor am I a hero when I travel in the company of others, but it makes me feel a lot more comfortable. During the events I have depicted in the stories I have had the company—in ever-changing combinations—of many colleagues and friends, among which: Eric Hedlund and Louise Weibul from Sweden, Delphine Resteigne and Audrey van Ouytsel from Belgium, Mussie Teclemichael Tessema from Eritrea, and many others from the Netherlands and elsewhere.

At several stages of the writing process I have kindly received encouragement, support, and useful suggestions from: Noel van Bemmel, Jan van der Meulen, Esmeralda Kleinreesink, Jacqueline Heeren-Bogers, Hume Johnson, Hans Dekkers and Eric Vrijsen. I have written these stories inspired by the always friendly incitements of the late Charlie Moskos, a leading military sociologist and very much a civilian traveller in the military himself. No one can ever tell, but I am pretty sure he would have liked this stuff. Alex, thanks, you will always be my teacher of English. Finally, whatever help and cooperation I have received from others, the responsibility for the final product is solely mine.

ENDNOTES

1   N. Van Bemmel (ed.), Task Force Uruzgan. Waargebeurde verhalen van onze soldaten (Task Force Uruzgan. True stories of our soldiers), Amsterdam: Meulenhoff, pages 233-237. In this version of the story several small changes have been made.

2   H. Murakami, Blind Willow. Sleeping Woman, New York: Vintage, 2006 (particularly the title story, pages 3-18).

3   See: P. Collier, Wars, Guns, and Votes. Democracy in Dangerous Places, New York etc.: Harper Perennial, 2009 (pages 239-240); also: A. Perry, Falling off the Edge. Globalization, World Peace and Other Lies, London: Pan Books, 2010.

4   R. Dallaire, Shake Hands with the Devil. The Failure of Humanity in Rwanda, London: Arrow Books, 2004, particularly pages 293-297 and 318.

5   Z. Smith, Changing My Mind. Occasional Essays, London: Hamish Hamilton, 2009 (particularly: One week in Liberia, pages 111-132).

6   A. Pierce, The Devil's Dictionary, London: Bloomsbury Publishing, 2003, page 66. R. Stewart, The Places In Between, Orlando etc.: Harcourt, Inc., 2006 (pages 20-21).

7   The general knowledge about racial relations in the U.S. armed forces is based on: Ch. Moskos and J. Sibley Butler, All that we can be. Black Leadership and Racial Integration the Army Way, New York: Basic Books, 1997. I have derived a number of nicknames in the U.S. Navy from: R.D. Kaplan, Hog Pilots, Blue Water Grunts. The American Military in the Air, at Sea, and on the Ground, New York, Vintage Books, 2007. The descriptions of the process of parking jet fighters on the deck of an aircraft carrier are from the famous article authored by Karl Weick and Karlene Robberts, Collective mind in organizations: heedful interrelating on flight decks, Administrative Science Quarterly,

1993, 38/3, 357-381, and those observations are partly based on: P.T. Gillcrist, Feet Wet Reflections of a Carrier, Novato CA: Presidio Press, 1990.

[8] J. Luther Long, Madame Butterfly, New York: The Century Co, 1904 (first publication: 1895).

[9] The most important reference has been the authoritative book by Joshua Levine, Beauty & Atrocity. People, Politics and Ireland's Fight for Peace, London: Collins, 2010. To get an idea of the experiences of the British soldiers: Ken Wharton, A Long, Long War. Voices from the British Army in Northern Ireland 1969-1998, Solihull: Helion & Cy, 2008. The story about the Afghan wedding party I took from: Dominic Streatfeild, A History of the World since 9/11, London: Atlantic Books (chapter 3).

[10] http://www.bloody-sunday-inquiry.org.

[11] The article referred to is: J. Kruger en D. Dunning, Unskilled and unaware of it: how difficulties in recognizing one's own incompetence lead to self-inflated self-assessments, Journal of Personality and Social Psychology, 1999 (77), pages 1121-1134. An application in the field of military history is: D.D.P. Johnson, Overconfidence and War. The Havoc and Glory of Positive Illusions, Cambridge, MA: Harvard UP, 2004. One can find a nice account of these phenomena in: Chr. Chabris and D. Simons, The Invisible Gorilla and Other Ways our Intuition Deceives Us, London: HarperCollins, 2011.